Third Edition

GREAT JOBS

FOR

Sociology Majors

Stephen Lambert

Mc
Graw
Hill

New York Chicago San Francisco Lisbon London Madrid Mexico City
Milan New Delhi San Juan Seoul Singapore Sydney Toronto

The *McGraw·Hill* Companies

Library of Congress Cataloging-in-Publication Data

Lambert, Stephen E.
  Great jobs for sociology majors / by Stephen Lambert. — 3rd ed.
      p.   cm.
  Includes bibliographical references and index.

  ISBN 978-0-07-183165-9

  1. Sociology—Vocational guidance—United States.   I. Title.

  HM585.L24   2008
  301.023′73—dc22   2008024666

1 2 3 4 5 6 7 8 9 10 11 12 13 14 15 16 17 18 19 20 21 22 23 24   DOC/DOC   0 9 8

MHID   0-07-154482-8

McGraw-Hill books are available at special quantity discounts to use as premiums and sales
promotions or for use in corporate training programs. To contact a representative, please visit the
Contact Us pages at www.mhprofessional.com.

This book is printed on acid-free paper.

This book is dedicated to my long-term colleagues at Plymouth State College. I want to express my deep gratitude for the pleasure of working alongside Steve Bamford, Diane Brandon, Gene Fahey, Michael Fischler, Dick and Pat Hage, Tim Keefe, Jim McLaughlin, Merryl Reichbach, and Bob Tuveson—my colleagues in the division of Student Affairs.

Writing this book, with its emphasis on the sociologist's fascination with how people and organizations function, has renewed my appreciation for the fine group of colleagues I have the opportunity to work with day in and day out on my campus.

The editors wish to thank Mark Rowh
for his assistance in preparing this revision.

Contents

Introduction

The Value of a Degree in Sociology

As a busy career counselor, I have spoken with many, many sociology majors throughout the years. Sociology has always been one of the more popular declared majors, and the number of students graduating with degrees in sociology and related social sciences is on the rise. It is striking how many of the students I talk with describe sociology as a "perfect fit" with who they are and what they want to learn. Sociology is an appealing field for several reasons, but perhaps one of the most compelling is that as a sociology major you are not just permitted but actively encouraged to pursue your questions about the social life of people. Few subjects could be as interesting, and few have a laboratory that encompasses every site of human interaction. We are social beings, and it follows that we would be intrigued by questions regarding our social relations, social structure and change, and the causes and consequences of human behavior.

Because sociology is the study of people in their social context, it calls for observing and studying the behavior of people as members of a group, rather than as individuals. If you're fascinated by groups and the behavior of people as social animals, the sociology major provides a deeply fulfilling course of study.

Sociology as a social science is a fairly recent development, growing out of a need to explain humankind's social behavior in a manner that was not addressed by other social sciences, such as history, economics, and political science. Economics studies the production and distribution of wealth. History addresses the problem of telling a factual, accurate story of what has happened in the past. And political science wrestles with questions regarding the distribution of power in society. Each examines human actions but from within their own discipline's framework. Sociology borrows from each of these fields but focuses on the study of people in social relationships. During the course of acquiring your degree in sociology, you develop a sense of history, as well as a good working knowledge of economics.

Sociology also touches closely upon the work of other disciplines. One of the closest working relationships is that between sociologists and statisticians who analyze the significance of sociological data. You'll examine the importance of this professional relationship when you study methods of social research.

Psychology and sociology have been so closely tied together that a specialization that incorporates both fields has evolved: social psychology. Social psychologists also acknowledge the contributions of both cultural anthropology and psychiatry. Psychologists attempt to understand individual human behavior, while sociologists try to discover basic truths about groups. When these two social sciences are combined, the focus is the study of persons as members of groups. Social psychologists study how individual behavior affects group behavior and the ways in which groups influence individual behavior. Sociologists and psychiatrists have also contributed to the efforts of the medical community.

Ethnology and ethnography, social sciences that treat the subdivisions of humankind and their description and classification, are other fields with which sociologists work closely. Problems in racial understanding and cooperation, in failures of communication, and in differences of belief and behavior are all concerns of the sociologist who studies underlying reasons for group conduct.

With all its strong ties to other fields of study, sociology is a very strong undergraduate preparation for many other careers: research, law, business, nursing, travel and tourism, and anthropology. It can not only provide a strong liberal arts background, but also foster an understanding of the human condition that can be brought to bear in many, many areas of employment or further education.

One additional way in which sociology develops you academically is through the synthesizing and generalizing that sociology does as it borrows from other disciplines.

In sum, as a sociology major, you have received an extremely strong foundation on which to build the career of your choice. With your understanding of social change and your well-developed research and communication skills, the real challenge ahead lies in deciding where you are most eager to apply your many talents.

Sociology Offers Unlimited Possibilities

The sociological inquiry focuses mainly on two areas: the social relationships or interactions of people in groups, and the role expectations or common beliefs and values people are likely to have about themselves and others within what they regard as "their" group.

As individuals, we often describe ourselves by letting others know what groups we belong to. Hence, part of our identity may be made up by our membership in a community safety board, a cross-country ski team, a sorority or fraternity, or a book club. It is an interesting exercise for sociology majors to put the groups we ourselves belong to under the microscope to examine how they work, who is friendly and who is not, and who is cooperative and who is competitive within the group. And while we may have a sense of why some individuals are singled out as leaders, how cliques form within a group, or how leaders treat members of the group, a rigorous sociological examination could reveal some elements that we had not yet taken into account. Do these exercises sound frivolous or unrelated to the pursuit of sociological knowledge? Not to a sociology major, who knows that these and many similar questions are what sociology is made of.

Another focus is to investigate the realm of values and beliefs. The attitudes and opinions that are held in common by group members are what bind them together and create the many smaller divisions within society as people cluster around commonly held beliefs. This can be quite complex, when ten members of a political party may belong to ten different religious organizations or have widely varying views on racial tolerance, birth control, education, or any number of subjects that they support through affiliation in other groups, with either active participation or simple identification with the aims of those groups.

Let's look at a standard description for an Introduction to Sociology course. At hundreds of colleges and universities around the country, new sociology students are enrolled in a class that covers something like this:

An introduction to the study of society that includes an examination of the issues of socialization, human interaction, social class, social inequality, human diversity, and social institutions.

This introductory course will paint, in broad brush strokes, the canvas of sociological study. You will begin by looking at the human world in the largest sense. You will become familiar with the sociological perspective on culture, society, how we "fit" in society (socialization), and the elements of personality.

You'll examine populations and how they move and why. Within those populations, you'll examine structures of class and hierarchies of esteem. You'll also examine communities, minorities, and the division of labor.

Much of your time will be spent looking at the social institutions of family, marriage, education, religion, and politics. You'll study social problems of child and spouse abuse, juvenile delinquency, and unemployment.

Each of the topics outlined in this introductory course is but the merest tip of an iceberg of information, study, research, and even subspecialties that are the life's work of sociologists around the world. Sociologists specialize in an array of focused areas. The following is a partial list of these:

- Penologists may specialize in research on the control and prevention of crime, punishment for crime and management of penal institutions, and rehabilitation of criminal offenders.
- Criminologists specialize in research on relationships between criminal law and social order in causes of crime and behavior of criminals.
- Industrial sociologists may specialize in research on group relationships and processes in an industrial organization.
- Rural sociologists may specialize in research on rural communities in contrast with urban communities and special problems occasioned by the impact of scientific and industrial revolutions on a rural way of life.
- Social ecologists specialize in research on interrelations between physical environment and technology in spatial distribution of people and their activities.
- Social problems specialists may specialize in research on social problems arising from individual or group deviation from commonly accepted standards of conduct, such as crime and delinquency, or social problems and racial discrimination rooted in the failure of society to achieve its collective purposes.
- Urban sociologists focus on research on the origin, growth, structure, and demographic characteristics of cities and social patterns and distinctive problems that result from an urban environment.

- Demographers are population specialists who collect and analyze vital statistics related to population changes, such as births, marriages, and deaths. Demographers plan and conduct demographic research, surveys, and experiments to study human populations and affecting trends.
- Clinical sociologists are concerned with group dysfunction and work with individuals and groups to identify and alleviate problems related to factors such as group organization, authority relationships, and role conflicts.
- Social pathologists specialize in investigation of group behavior that is considered detrimental to the proper functioning of society.
- Social welfare research workers conduct research that is used as a tool for planning and carrying out social welfare programs.

This list hardly makes a dent in the possible fields of study that can engage or will engage the sociologist of the future. The sociologist is in the very middle of our culture. Those who enjoy analyzing the meaning of current trends should enjoy thoroughly the professional experiences of sociology.

Many of these specialties demand an advanced degree. For many positions, those with a master's degree or Ph.D. will be more likely to get job offers than those with bachelor's degrees. Nevertheless, possibilities for entering the field still exist for the persistent applicant. For example, one can start with a job in a research organization as an interviewer—a typical entry-level position. Or you might assist in other ways with the collection of data. Begin immediately to acquire as many of those "portable skills" offered in your workplace as you can, including computer applications, training, leadership opportunities, and writing assignments. Use any educational benefits offered to begin acquiring the educational background you feel will move you forward in your career.

If you've selected sociology simply because you want a degree that promises the most mileage from your investment in a college education, sociology delivers! Many new graduates will be hired as trainees and assistants in business, industry, and government, where once again, the outlook is best for those with training in quantitative research methods. Some with a bachelor's degree may obtain work in social welfare agencies.

A sociology major is also a fantastic way to launch yourself into other related careers. Many people choose to major in sociology because of the strong preparation it gives them for fields such as journalism, law, business, social work, recreation, and counseling. With the proper state certification, you may even teach sociology in high schools.

Sociologists also have a noticeable role in a number of federal government agencies, a career path that is discussed in detail in this guide. While many government sociologists work in research, others are active in administering a number of federal programs, while another whole subset functions in an advisory capacity. And in the private sphere, some individuals may be employed by private research organizations while others contribute their sociological expertise to management consultant firms.

Whether you are determined to enter the workforce right away or are considering a graduate degree in sociology, it will be immensely helpful to your own self-awareness and for your résumé to think about doing an internship. Whether you are still in college or pursuing an internship upon graduation, the intern experience will allow you to try on a potential career to see if it fits. Though many internships do not pay, the dividends can still be enormous, as they increase your chances of admission to graduate school (should that be your destination) as well as your ability to get the next job. As you may well know, entry-level positions are often advertised for those who have both a degree as well as a year or two of actual work experience. An internship not only allows you to fine-tune your own career search, but also opens doors that might otherwise remain closed.

The World We Live In

Thoreau's *Walden* remains a popular book, even though it was written between 1846 and 1847. Part of its attractiveness is probably our yearning to live in a simpler, less complex society. The reality is that we do not. In fact, many would argue that society is becoming bewilderingly complex. All of us, no matter what our major, would do well to learn a great deal about the society and world we live in. It is the only antidote to prejudice or sentiment. Sociology's promise is to replace blind sentiment and thoughtless prejudice with sociological knowledge. This is especially important in a democratic country such as ours where there are so many choices and legal protections for those choices.

All of our major adjustments in life, including the important transitions into and out of college, are far easier if we understand and appreciate how society and its trends work. How are organizations structured, and how can you make your own way in them? What is the current dialogue on privacy and freedom of choice, and what effect does that have on your role as a worker? Are societal shifts temporary, or is there some long-term trend occurring? The answers don't lie in this book, but for the student embarking on a study of sociology, these and many other questions will provide the beginnings of a wonderful, possibly lifelong dialogue. Sociology will fulfill the promise of a lifetime of excitement, discovery, and satisfaction.

PART ONE

THE JOB SEARCH

1

The Self-Assessment

Self-assessment is the process by which you begin to acknowledge your own particular blend of education, experiences, values, needs, and goals. It provides the foundation for career planning and the entire job search process. Self-assessment involves looking inward and asking yourself what can sometimes prove to be difficult questions. This self-examination should lead to an intimate understanding of your personal traits and values, consumption patterns and economic needs, longer-term goals, skill base, preferred skills, and underdeveloped skills.

You come to the self-assessment process knowing yourself well in some of these areas, but you may still be uncertain about other aspects. You may be well aware of your consumption patterns, but have you spent much time specifically identifying your longer-term goals or your personal values as they relate to work? No matter what level of self-assessment you have undertaken to date, it is now time to clarify all of these issues and questions as they relate to the job search.

The knowledge you gain in the self-assessment process will guide the rest of your job search. In this book, you will learn about all of the following tasks:

- Writing résumés and cover letters
- Researching careers and networking
- Interviewing and job offer considerations

In each of these steps, you will rely on and often return to the understanding gained through your self-assessment. Any individual seeking employment must be able and willing to express these facets of his or her personality to recruiters and interviewers throughout the job search. This communication allows you to show the world who you are so that together with employers you can determine whether there will be a workable match with a given job or career path.

How to Conduct a Self-Assessment

The self-assessment process goes on naturally all the time. People ask you to clarify what you mean, you make a purchasing decision, or you begin a new relationship. You react to the world and the world reacts to you. How you understand these interactions and any changes you might make because of them are part of the natural process of self-discovery. There is, however, a more comprehensive and efficient way to approach self-assessment with regard to employment.

Because self-assessment can become a complex exercise, we have distilled it into a seven-step process that provides an effective basis for undertaking a job search. The seven steps include the following:

1. Understanding your personal traits
2. Identifying your personal values
3. Calculating your economic needs
4. Exploring your longer-term goals
5. Enumerating your skill base
6. Recognizing your preferred skills
7. Assessing skills needing further development

As you work through your self-assessment, you might want to create a worksheet similar to the one shown in Exhibit 1.1, starting on the following page. Or you might want to keep a journal of the thoughts you have as you undergo this process. There will be many opportunities to revise your self-assessment as you start down the path of seeking a career.

Step 1   Understand Your Personal Traits

Each person has a unique personality that he or she brings to the job search process. Gaining a better understanding of your personal traits can help you evaluate job and career choices. Identifying these traits and then finding employment that allows you to draw on at least some of them can create a rewarding and fulfilling work experience. If potential employment doesn't allow you to use these preferred traits, it is important to decide whether you

Exhibit 1.1
SELF-ASSESSMENT WORKSHEET

Step 1. Understand Your Personal Traits

The personal traits that describe me are
(Include all of the words that describe you.)
The ten personal traits that most accurately describe me are
(List these ten traits.)

Step 2. Identify Your Personal Values

Working conditions that are important to me include
(List working conditions that would have to exist for you to accept a position.)
The values that go along with my working conditions are
(Write down the values that correspond to each working condition.)
Some additional values I've decided to include are
(List those values you identify as you conduct this job search.)

Step 3. Calculate Your Economic Needs

My estimated minimum annual salary requirement is
(Write the salary you have calculated based on your budget.)
Starting salaries for the positions I'm considering are
(List the name of each job you are considering and the associated starting salary.)

Step 4. Explore Your Longer-Term Goals

My thoughts on longer-term goals right now are
(Jot down some of your longer-term goals as you know them right now.)

Step 5. Enumerate Your Skill Base

The general skills I possess are
(List the skills that underlie tasks you are able to complete.)
The specific skills I possess are
(List more technical or specific skills that you possess, and indicate your level of expertise.)
General and specific skills that I want to promote to employers for the jobs I'm considering are
(List general and specific skills for each type of job you are considering.)

continued

Step 6. Recognize Your Preferred Skills

Skills that I would like to use on the job include

(List skills that you hope to use on the job, and indicate how often you'd like to use them.)

Step 7. Assess Skills Needing Further Development

Some skills that I'll need to acquire for the jobs I'm considering include

(Write down skills listed in job advertisements or job descriptions that you don't currently possess.)

I believe I can build these skills by

(Describe how you plan to acquire these skills.)

---

can find other ways to express them or whether you would be better off not considering this type of job. Interests and hobbies pursued outside of work hours can be one way to use personal traits you don't have an opportunity to draw on in your work. For example, if you consider yourself an outgoing person and the kinds of jobs you are examining allow little contact with other people, you may be able to achieve the level of interaction that is comfortable for you outside of your work setting. If such a compromise seems impractical or otherwise unsatisfactory, you probably should explore only jobs that provide the interaction you want and need on the job.

Many young adults who are not very confident about their employability will downplay their need for income. They will say, "Money is not all that important if I love my work." But if you begin to document exactly what you need for housing, transportation, insurance, clothing, food, and utilities, you will begin to understand that some jobs cannot meet your financial needs and it doesn't matter how wonderful the job is. If you have to worry each payday about bills and other financial obligations, you won't be very effective on the job. Begin now to be honest with yourself about your needs.

Begin the self-assessment process by creating an inventory of your personal traits. Make a list of as many words as possible to describe yourself. Words like *accurate, creative, future-oriented, relaxed,* or *structured* are just a few examples. In addition, you might ask people who know you well how they might describe you.

Focus on Selected Personal Traits. Of all the traits you identified, select the ten you believe most accurately describe you. Keep track of these ten traits.

Consider Your Personal Traits in the Job Search Process. As you begin exploring jobs and careers, watch for matches between your personal traits and the job descriptions you read. Some jobs will require many personal traits you know you possess, and others will not seem to match those traits.

Professors, for example, must interact regularly with students and colleagues to carry out their academic work. They need strong writing and speaking skills, imagination, good interpersonal skills, and the ability to listen well. They must enjoy talking with people and answering questions, and they must become skilled at presenting information using a variety of methods to appeal to different types of learners. An analyst's work, on the other hand, requires attention to detail, self-discipline, motivation, and the ability to deal with different kinds of information, including both statistical data and narrative material. Analysts may focus on the same project for an extended period of time. They often work alone, with limited opportunities for interacting with other people.

Your ability to respond to changing conditions, your decision-making ability, productivity, creativity, and verbal skills all have a bearing on your success in and enjoyment of your work life. To better guarantee success, be sure to take the time needed to understand these traits in yourself.

Step 2 Identify Your Personal Values
Your personal values affect every aspect of your life, including employment, and they develop and change as you move through life. Values can be defined as principles that we hold in high regard, qualities that are important and desirable to us. Some values aren't ordinarily connected to work (love, beauty, color, light, relationships, family, or religion), and others are (autonomy, cooperation, effectiveness, achievement, knowledge, and security). Our values determine, in part, the level of satisfaction we feel in a particular job.

Define Acceptable Working Conditions. One facet of employment is the set of working conditions that must exist for someone to consider taking a job.

Each of us would probably create a unique list of acceptable working conditions, but items that might be included on many people's lists are the amount of money you would need to be paid, how far you are willing to drive or travel, the amount of freedom you want in determining your own schedule, whether you would be working with people or data or things, and the types of tasks you would be willing to do. Your conditions might include statements of working conditions you will *not* accept; for example, you might not be willing to work at night or on weekends or holidays.

If you were offered a job tomorrow, what conditions would have to exist for you to realistically consider accepting the position? Take some time and make a list of these conditions.

Realize Associated Values. Your list of working conditions can be used to create an inventory of your values relating to jobs and careers you are exploring. For example, if one of your conditions stated that you wanted to earn at least $30,000 per year, the associated value would be financial gain. If another condition was that you wanted to work with a friendly group of people, the value that went along with that might be belonging or interaction with people.

Relate Your Values to the World of Work. As you read the job descriptions you come across either in this book, in newspapers and magazines, or online, think about the values associated with each position.

For instance, the work of a human resources director would include planning the work of office support staff and developing overall plans for the office's work in supporting the organization. As support staff are carrying out assigned tasks, the director must supervise their efforts and evaluate their progress in meeting office goals.

At least some of the associated values in the field you're exploring should match those you extracted from your list of working conditions. Take a second look at any values that don't match up. How important are they to you? What will happen if they are not satisfied on the job? Can you incorporate those personal values elsewhere? Your answers need to be brutally honest. As you continue your exploration, be sure to add to your list any additional values that occur to you.

Step 3 Calculate Your Economic Needs

Each of us grew up in an environment that provided for certain basic needs, such as food and shelter, and, to varying degrees, other needs that we now consider basic, such as cable television, e-mail, or an automobile. Needs such as privacy, space, and quiet, which at first glance may not appear to be monetary needs, may add to housing expenses and so should be considered as you examine your economic needs. For example, if you place a high value on a large, open living space for yourself, it would be difficult to satisfy that need without an associated high housing cost, especially in a densely populated city environment.

As you prepare to move into the world of work and become responsible for meeting your own basic needs, it is important to consider the salary you will need to be able to afford a satisfying standard of living. The three-step process outlined here will help you plan a budget, which in turn will allow you to evaluate the various career choices and geographic locations you are considering. The steps include (1) develop a realistic budget, (2) examine starting salaries, and (3) use a cost-of-living index.

Develop a Realistic Budget. Each of us has certain expectations for the kind of lifestyle we want to maintain. To begin the process of defining your economic needs, it will be helpful to determine what you expect to spend on routine monthly expenses. These expenses include housing, food, transportation, entertainment, utilities, loan repayments, and revolving charge accounts. You may not currently spend anything for certain items, but you probably will have to once you begin supporting yourself. As you develop this budget, be generous in your estimates, but keep in mind any items that could be reduced or eliminated. If you are not sure about the cost of a certain item, talk with family or friends who would be able to give you a realistic estimate.

If this is new or difficult for you, start to keep a log of expenses right now. You may be surprised at how much you actually spend each month for food or stamps or magazines. Household expenses and personal grooming items can often loom very large in a budget, as can auto repairs or home maintenance.

Income taxes must also be taken into consideration when examining salary requirements. State and local taxes vary, so it is difficult to calculate exactly the effect of taxes on the amount of income you need to generate. To roughly estimate the gross income necessary to generate your minimum annual salary requirement, multiply the minimum salary you have calculated by a factor of 1.35. The resulting figure will be an approximation of what your gross income would need to be, given your estimated expenses.

Examine Starting Salaries. Starting salaries for each of the career tracks are provided throughout this book. These salary figures can be used in conjunction with the cost-of-living index (discussed in the next section) to determine whether you would be able to meet your basic economic needs in a given geographic location.

Use a Cost-of-Living Index. If you are thinking about trying to get a job in a geographic region other than the one where you now live, understanding differences in the cost of living will help you come to a more informed decision about making a move. By using a cost-of-living index, you can compare salaries offered and the cost of living in different locations with what you know about the salaries offered and the cost of living in your present location.

Many variables are used to calculate the cost-of-living index. Often included are housing, groceries, utilities, transportation, health care, clothing, and entertainment expenses. Right now you do not need to worry about the details associated with calculating a given index. The main purpose of this exercise is to help you understand that pay ranges for entry-level positions may not vary greatly, but the cost of living in different locations *can* vary tremendously.

If you lived in Charlotte, North Carolina, for example, and you were interested in working as a social worker, you might find that you would earn $45,000 annually. But let's say you're also thinking about moving to San Diego, California; Gary, Indiana; or Lexington, Kentucky. You know you can live on $45,000 in Charlotte, but you want to be able to equal that salary in the other locations you're considering. How much will you have to earn in those locations to do this? Determining the cost of living for each city will show you. There are many websites, such as DataMasters (datamasters.com), that can assist you as you undertake this research. Or use any search engine and enter the keywords *cost-of-living index*. Several choices will appear. Choose one site and look for options like cost-of-living analysis or cost-of-living comparator. Some sites will ask you to register and/or pay for the information, but most sites are free. Follow the instructions provided and you will be able to create a table of information like the one on page 11. At the time this comparison was done, you would have needed to earn $58,287 in San Diego, $49,533 in Gary, or just $43,709 in Lexington to match the buying power of $45,000 in Charlotte.

JOB: SOCIAL WORKER		
City	**Base Amount**	**Equivalent Salary**
Charlotte, NC	$45,000	
San Diego, CA		$58,287
Gary, IN		$49,533
Lexington, KY		$43,709

If you would like to determine whether it's financially worthwhile to make any of these moves, it's also helpful to know the salaries that might be expected for social work positions in other locations. To obtain an idea of what to expect, you might consider steps such as the following:

- Check out online job sites such as Salary.com and Monster.com.
- Consult want ads of newspapers in cities in which you are interested.
- Write or call colleagues who are already working in the region and ask if they will share information about salary ranges (not specific salaries, which may be considered personal or confidential).
- Contact executive directors or human resources officers at organizations that employ social workers and request general salary ranges.
- Contact college or university career services offices.
- Check out salaries in comparable (if not directly related) positions.

If you moved to Lexington and secured employment as a social worker with the same salary you earned in Charlotte, you would be able to maintain a lifestyle similar to the one you lead in North Carolina. In fact, you would be able to enhance your lifestyle modestly given the slight increase in buying power. On the other hand, moving to Gary from Charlotte would decrease your buying power unless your new salary was at least $49,500. And without a significantly larger increase (to at least $58,000), moving to San Diego would mean a more drastic change in your buying power. Remember, these figures change all the time, so be sure to undertake your own calculations. If you would like to see how the figures were calculated, you can visit the website mentioned above (datamasters.com). Or check out other sites that provide cost-of-living comparisons.

You can work through a similar exercise for any type of job you are considering and for many locations when current salary information is available. It will be worth your time to undertake this analysis if you are seriously considering a relocation. By doing so you will be able to make an informed choice.

Step 4 Explore Your Longer-Term Goals

There is no question that when we first begin working, our goals are to use our skills and education in a job that will reward us with employment, income, and status relative to the preparation we brought with us to this position. If we are not being paid as much as we feel we should for our level of education or if job demands don't provide the intellectual stimulation we had hoped for, we experience unhappiness and as a result often seek other employment.

Most jobs we consider "good" are those that fulfill our basic "lower-level" needs of security, food, clothing, shelter, income, and productive work. But even when our basic needs are met and our jobs are secure and productive, we as individuals are constantly changing. As we change, the demands and expectations we place on our jobs may change. Fortunately, some jobs grow and change with us, and this explains why some people are happy throughout many years in a job.

But more often people are bigger than the jobs they fill. We have more goals and needs than any job could satisfy. These are "higher-level" needs of self-esteem, companionship, affection, and an increasing desire to feel we are employing ourselves in the most effective way possible. Not all of these higher-level needs can be met through employment, but for as long as we are employed, we increasingly demand that our jobs play their part in moving us along the path to fulfillment.

Another obvious but important fact is that we change as we mature. Although our jobs also have the potential for change, they may not change as frequently or as markedly as we do. There are increasingly fewer one-job, one-employer careers; we must think about a work future that may involve voluntary or forced moves from employer to employer. Because of that very real possibility, we need to take advantage of the opportunities in each position we hold. Acquiring the skills and competencies associated with each position will keep us viable and attractive as employees. This is particularly true in a job market that not only is technology/computer dependent, but also is populated with more and more small, self-transforming organizations rather than the large, seemingly stable organizations of the past.

If you are considering the possibility of working as a college professor of sociology, for example, you would gain a better perspective of your potential future if you talked to a graduate assistant or first-year instructor at a college or university, an assistant or associate professor at a community college or small four-year school, and finally a full professor or department chairperson at a medium-sized or large university with significant experience in both teaching and research. Each person will be able to offer advice based on his or her different experiences and outlook.

Step 5   Enumerate Your Skill Base

In terms of the job search, skills can be thought of as capabilities that can be developed in school, at work, or by volunteering and then used in specific job settings. Many studies have documented the kinds of skills that employers seek in entry-level applicants. For example, some of the most desired skills for individuals interested in the teaching profession are the ability to interact effectively with students one-on-one, to manage a classroom, to adapt to varying situations as necessary, and to get involved in school activities. Business employers have also identified important qualities, including enthusiasm for the employer's product or service, a businesslike mind, the ability to follow written or oral instructions, the ability to demonstrate self-control, the confidence to suggest new ideas, the ability to communicate with all members of a group, an awareness of cultural differences, and loyalty, to name just a few. You will find that many of these skills are also in the repertoire of qualities demanded in your college major.

To be successful in obtaining any given job, you must be able to demonstrate that you possess a certain mix of skills that will allow you to carry out the duties required by that job. This skill mix will vary a great deal from job to job; to determine the skills necessary for the jobs you are seeking, you can read job advertisements or more generic job descriptions, such as those found later in this book. If you want to be effective in the job search, you must directly show employers that you possess the skills needed to be successful in filling the position. These skills will initially be described on your résumé and then discussed again during the interview process.

Skills are either general or specific. To develop a list of skills relevant to employers, you must first identify the general skills you possess, then list specific skills you have to offer, and, finally, examine which of these skills employers are seeking.

Identify Your General Skills. Because you possess or will possess a college degree, employers will assume that you can read and write, perform certain basic computations, think critically, and communicate effectively. Employers will want to see that you have acquired these skills, and they will want to know which additional general skills you possess.

One way to begin identifying skills is to write an experiential diary. An experiential diary lists all the tasks you were responsible for completing for each job you've held and then outlines the skills required to do those tasks. You may list several skills for any given task. This diary allows you to distinguish between the tasks you performed and the underlying skills required to complete those tasks. Here's an example:

Tasks	Skills
Circuit design	Use of basic test equipment (voltmeter, oscilloscope, etc.) to take test data and troubleshoot problems
Programming industrial controls	PLC experience
Presentations to engineering teams	Organization of thoughts and clear communication skills

For each job or experience you have participated in, develop a worksheet based on the example shown here. On a résumé, you may want to describe these skills rather than simply listing tasks. Skills are easier for the employer to appreciate, especially when your experience is very different from the employment you are seeking. In addition to helping you identify general skills, this experiential diary will prepare you to speak more effectively in an interview about the qualifications you possess.

Identify Your Specific Skills. It may be easier to identify your specific skills because you can definitely say whether you can speak other languages, program a computer, draft a map or diagram, or edit a document using appropriate symbols and terminology.

Using your experiential diary, identify the points in your history where you learned how to do something very specific, and decide whether you have a beginning, intermediate, or advanced knowledge of how to use that particular skill. Right now, be sure to list *every* specific skill you have, and don't consider whether you like using the skill. Write down a list of specific skills you have acquired and the level of competence you possess—beginning, intermediate, or advanced.

Relate Your Skills to Employers. You probably have thought about a couple of different jobs you might be interested in obtaining, and one way to begin relating the general and specific skills you possess to a potential employer's needs is to read actual advertisements for these types of positions (see Part Two for resources listing actual job openings).

For instance, perhaps you would be interested in starting your career as a human resources assistant, working in a large organization where there is room for advancement. A job listing for a human resources assistant might read, "Assist director in providing basic support in a full-service human resources office. Requires bachelor's degree, excellent writing skills, organizational capabilities, communication/presentation skills, and word-processing capabilities." If you then used any one of a number of general sources of information that describe the job of human resources assistant, you would find additional information. Workers in this area might process job applications, record leave requests, assist in payroll processing, or write employee newsletters or other informational materials.

Start building a comprehensive list of required skills with the first job description you read. Exploring advertisements for and descriptions of several types of related positions will reveal an important core of skills that are necessary for obtaining the type of work you're interested in. In building this list, include both general and specific skills.

Following is a sample list of skills needed to be successful as a human resources assistant. These items were extracted from both general resources and actual job listings.

JOB: HUMAN RESOURCES ASSISTANT

General Skills	Specific Skills
Review documents	Summarize personnel information
Perform interviews	Analyze benefit plans
Draft informational	Set up interview schedules
materials	Develop newsletters
Draft correspondence	Write job descriptions
Organize files	Develop job postings
Conduct studies	Communicate effectively
Search sources	Summarize hiring trends
Use computer	Use phone extensively
Present information	Keep written records
orally	Work under pressure
Answer inquiries	Use computer software
	Conduct oral interviews

On separate sheets of paper or computer files, try to generate a comprehensive list of required skills for at least one job you are considering.

The list of general skills that you develop for a given career path will be valuable for any number of jobs you might apply for. Many of the specific skills would also be transferable to other types of positions. For example, writing informational materials is a required skill for many positions.

Step 6 Recognize Your Preferred Skills

In the previous section you developed a comprehensive list of skills that relate to particular career paths that are of interest to you. You can now relate these to skills that you prefer to use. We all use a wide range of skills (some researchers say individuals have a repertoire of about five hundred skills), but we may not particularly be interested in using all of them in our work. There may be some skills that come to us more naturally or that we use successfully time and time again and that we want to continue to use; these are best described as our preferred skills. For this exercise use the list of skills that you created for the previous section, and decide which of them you are *most interested in using* in future work and how often you would like to use them. You might be interested in using some skills only occasionally, while others you would like to use more regularly. You probably also have skills that you hope you can use constantly.

As you examine job announcements, look for matches between this list of preferred skills and the qualifications described in the advertisements. These skills should be highlighted on your résumé and discussed in job interviews.

Step 7 Assess Skills Needing Further Development

Previously you compiled a list of general and specific skills required for given positions. You already possess some of these skills; those that remain to be developed are your underdeveloped skills.

If you are just beginning the job search, there may be gaps between the qualifications required for some of the jobs you're considering and the skills you possess. The thought of having to admit to and talk about these underdeveloped skills, especially in a job interview, is a frightening one. One way to put a healthy perspective on this subject is to target and relate your exploration of underdeveloped skills to the types of positions you are seeking. Recognizing these shortcomings and planning to overcome them with either on-the-job training or additional formal education can be a positive way to address the concept of underdeveloped skills.

On your worksheet or in your journal, make a list of up to five general or specific skills required for the positions you're interested in that you *don't currently possess*. For each item list an idea you have for specific action you could take to acquire that skill. Do some brainstorming to come up with possible actions. If you have a hard time generating ideas, talk to people currently working in this type of position, professionals in your college career services office, trusted friends, family members, or members of related professional associations.

In the chapter on interviewing, we will discuss in detail how to effectively address questions about underdeveloped skills. Generally speaking, though, employers want genuine answers to these types of questions. They want you to reveal "the real you," and they also want to see how you answer difficult questions. In taking the positive, targeted approach discussed previously, you show the employer that you are willing to continue to learn and that you have a plan for strengthening your job qualifications.

Use Your Self-Assessment

Exploring entry-level career options can be an exciting experience if you have good resources available and will take the time to use them. Can you effectively complete the following tasks?

1. Understand your personality traits and relate them to career choices
2. Define your personal values
3. Determine your economic needs
4. Explore longer-term goals
5. Understand your skill base
6. Recognize your preferred skills
7. Express a willingness to improve on your underdeveloped skills

If so, then you can more meaningfully participate in the job search process by writing a more effective résumé, finding job titles that represent work you are interested in doing, locating job sites that will provide the opportunity for you to use your strengths and skills, networking in an informed way, participating in focused interviews, getting the most out of follow-up contacts, and evaluating job offers to find those that create a good match between you and the employer. The remaining chapters in Part One guide you through these next steps in the job search process. For many job seekers, this process can take anywhere from three months to a year to implement. The time you will need to put into your job search will depend on the type of job you want and the geographic location where you'd like to work. Think of your effort as a job in itself, requiring you to set aside time each week to complete the needed work. Carefully undertaken efforts may reduce the time you need for your job search.

2

The Résumé and Cover Letter

The task of writing a résumé may seem overwhelming if you are unfamiliar with this type of document, but there are some easily understood techniques that can and should be used. This section was written to help you understand the purpose of the résumé, the different types of formats available, and how to write the sections that contain information traditionally found on a résumé. We will present examples and explanations that address questions frequently posed by people writing their first résumé or updating an old one.

Even within the formats and suggestions given, however, there are infinite variations. True, most follow one of the outlines suggested, but you should feel free to adjust the résumé to suit your needs and make it expressive of your life and experience.

Why Write a Résumé?

The purpose of a résumé is to convince an employer that you should be interviewed. Whether you're mailing, faxing, or e-mailing this document, you'll want to present enough information to show that you can make an immediate and valuable contribution to an organization. A résumé is not an indepth historical or legal document; later in the job search process you may be asked to document your entire work history on an application form and attest to its validity. The résumé should, instead, highlight relevant information pertaining directly to the organization that will receive the document or to the type of position you are seeking.

We will discuss the chronological and digital résumés in detail here. Functional and targeted résumés, which are used much less often, are briefly discussed. The reasons for using one type of résumé over another and the typical format for each are addressed in the following sections.

The Chronological Résumé

The chronological résumé is the most common of the various résumé formats and therefore the format that employers are most used to receiving. This type of résumé is easy to read and understand because it details the chronological progression of jobs you have held. (See Exhibit 2.1.) It begins with your most recent employment and works back in time. If you have a solid work history or have experience that provided growth and development in your duties and responsibilities, a chronological résumé will highlight these achievements. The typical elements of a chronological résumé include the heading, a career objective, educational background, employment experience, activities, and references.

The Heading
The heading consists of your name, address, telephone number, and other means of contact. This may include a fax number, e-mail address, and your home-page address. If you are using a shared e-mail account or a parent's business fax, be sure to let others who use these systems know that you may receive important professional correspondence via these systems. You wouldn't want to miss a vital e-mail or fax! Likewise, if your résumé directs readers to a personal home page on the Web, be certain it's a professional personal home page designed to be viewed and appreciated by a prospective employer. This may mean making substantial changes in the home page you currently mount on the Web.

The Objective
Without a doubt the objective statement is the most challenging part of the résumé for most writers. Even for individuals who have decided on a career path, it can be difficult to encapsulate all they want to say in one or two brief sentences. For job seekers who are unfocused or unclear about their intentions, trying to write this section can inhibit the entire résumé writing process.

Keep the objective as short as possible and no longer than two short sentences.

Exhibit 2.1
CHRONOLOGICAL RÉSUMÉ

KIRSTEN L. COX

2321 Walker Street	6512 Citadel Place
Tallahassee, FL 32308	Charleston, SC 29465
(813) 555-8645 (mobile)	(843) 555-1836
kirsten77@xxx.net	
(until May 2009)	

OBJECTIVE
Challenging position in human resources or a related area

EDUCATION
Bachelor of Arts in Sociology
Florida State University
Major: Sociology
Minor: Business Administration

HONORS/AWARDS
Outstanding Sociology Student, 2008
Dean's List, eight semesters
Smallwood Undergraduate Research Award, 2008
Golden Frond Honor Society

RELATED COURSES

Human Resource Management	Business Communications
Organizational Psychology	32 credits in Sociology

EXPERIENCE
Work-Study Student, Florida State University, 2006–2008
Assisted chairperson of Department of Sociology and Anthropology in general
    office management and clerical tasks.

Customer Service Representative, FSU Health and Recreation Center, 2006–2007
Assisted students in signing up for noncredit classes and special services.
    Checked out recreation equipment for student and community use.

continued

Operated telephone system, computers, and other office equipment.
Developed new inventory tracking system.

Intern, Southern Association of Human Resources Officers, Charleston, SC,
Summer 2007
Assisted in planning annual conference and other meetings. Reviewed and
updated membership directory. Redesigned association website. Assisted in
updating of brochures describing association policies and services.

ACTIVITIES
Students in Sociology Association
Women's Resource Center Volunteer
Newsletter editor, Campus United Way Campaign

REFERENCES
Available upon request

Choose one of the following types of objective statement:

1. *General Objective Statement*

- An entry-level educational programming coordinator position

2. *Position-Focused Objective*

- To obtain the position of conference coordinator at State College

3. *Industry-Focused Objective*

- To begin a career as a sales representative in the cruise line industry

4. *Summary of Qualifications Statement*

My two years of experience in marketing research and my internship with a major research firm have prepared me to take on
the responsibilities of a full-time research analyst.

Support Your Objective. A résumé that contains any one of these types of objective statements should then go on to demonstrate why you are qualified to get the position. Listing academic degrees can be one way to indicate qualifications. Another demonstration would be in the way previous experiences, both volunteer and paid, are described. Without this kind of documentation in the body of the résumé, the objective looks unsupported. Think of the résumé as telling a connected story about you. All the elements should work together to form a coherent picture that ideally should relate to your statement of objective.

Education

This section of your résumé should indicate the exact name of the degree you will receive or have received, spelled out completely with no abbreviations. The degree is generally listed after the objective, followed by the institution name and location, and then the month and year of graduation. This section could also include your academic minor, grade point average (GPA), and appearance on the Dean's List or President's List.

If you have enough space, you might want to include a section listing courses related to the field in which you are seeking work. The best use of a "related courses" section would be to list some course work that is not traditionally associated with the major. Perhaps you took several computer courses outside your degree that will be helpful and related to the job prospects you are entertaining. A couple of education section examples are shown here:

- B.S in Sociology with a minor in Anthropology, Ohio University, Athens, OH; May 2009
- Bachelor of Arts degree in Sociology, University of Texas, Austin, TX; August 2009; Concentration: Social Research and Statistics

An example of a format for a related courses section follows:

RELATED COURSES

Public Relations	Web Design
Marketing Research	Desktop Publishing
Public Speaking	Expository Writing
Statistics & Research Design	

Experience

The experience section of your résumé should be the most substantial part and should take up most of the space on the page. Employers want to see what kind of work history you have. They will look at your range of experiences, longevity in jobs, and specific tasks you are able to complete. This section may also be called "work experience," "related experience," "employment history," or "employment." No matter what you call this section, some important points to remember are the following:

1. **Describe your duties** as they relate to the position you are seeking.
2. **Emphasize major responsibilities** and indicate increases in responsibility. Include all relevant employment experiences: summer, part-time, internships, cooperative education, or self-employment.
3. **Emphasize skills**, especially those that transfer from one situation to another. The fact that you coordinated a student organization, chaired meetings, supervised others, and managed a budget leads one to suspect that you could coordinate other things as well.
4. **Use descriptive job titles** that provide information about what you did. A "Student Intern" should be more specifically stated as, for example, "Magazine Operations Intern." "Volunteer" is also too general; a title such as "Peer Writing Tutor" would be more appropriate.
5. **Create word pictures** by using active verbs to start sentences. Describe *results* you have produced in the work you have done.

A limp description would say something such as the following: "My duties included helping with production, proofreading, and editing. I used a design and page layout program." An action statement would be stated as follows: "Coordinated and assisted in the creative marketing of brochures and seminar promotions, becoming proficient in Quark."

Remember, an accomplishment is simply a result, a final measurable product that people can relate to. A duty is not a result; it is an obligation—every job holder has duties. For an effective résumé, list as many results as you can. To make the most of the limited space you have and to give your description impact, carefully select appropriate and accurate descriptors.

Here are some traits that employers tell us they like to see:

- Teamwork
- Energy and motivation

- Learning and using new skills
- Versatility
- Critical thinking
- Understanding how profits are created
- Organizational acumen
- Risk taking
- Communicating directly and clearly, in both writing and speaking
- Willingness to admit mistakes
- High personal standards

Solutions to Frequently Encountered Problems

Repetitive Employment with the Same Employer
EMPLOYMENT: The Foot Locker, Portland, Oregon. Summer 2001, 2002, 2003. Initially employed in high school as salesclerk. Because of successful performance, asked to return next two summers at higher pay with added responsibility. Ranked as the #2 salesperson the first summer and #1 the next two summers. Assisted in arranging eye-catching retail displays; served as manager of other summer workers during owner's absence.

A Large Number of Jobs
EMPLOYMENT: Recent Hospitality Industry Experience: Affiliated with four upscale hotel/restaurant complexes (September 2001–February 2004), where I worked part- and full-time as a waiter, bartender, disc jockey, and bookkeeper to produce income for college.

Several Positions with the Same Employer
EMPLOYMENT: Coca-Cola Bottling Co., Burlington, Vermont, 2001–2004. In four years, I received three promotions, each with increased pay and responsibility.

Summer Sales Coordinator: Promoted to hire, train, and direct efforts of add-on staff of fifteen college-age route salespeople hired to meet summer peak demand for product.

Sales Administrator: Promoted to run home office sales desk, managing accounts and associated delivery schedules for professional sales force of ten people. Intensive phone work, daily interaction with all personnel, and strong knowledge of product line required.

Route Salesperson: Summer employment to travel and tourism industry sites that use Coke products. Met specific schedule demands, used good communication skills with wide variety of customers, and demonstrated strong selling skills. Named salesperson of the month for July and August of that year.

Questions Résumé Writers Often Ask

How Far Back Should I Go in Terms of Listing Past Jobs?
Usually, listing three or four jobs should suffice. If you did something back in high school that has a bearing on your future aspirations for employment, by all means list the job. As you progress through your college career, high school jobs will be replaced on the résumé by college employment.

Should I Differentiate Between Paid and Nonpaid Employment?
Most employers are not initially concerned about how much you were paid. They are eager to know how much responsibility you held in your past employment. There is no need to specify that your work was as a volunteer if you had significant responsibilities.

How Should I Represent My Accomplishments or Work-Related Responsibilities?
Succinctly, but fully. In other words, give the employer enough information to arouse curiosity but not so much detail that you leave nothing to the imagination. Besides, some jobs merit more lengthy explanations than others. Be sure to convey any information that can give an employer a better understanding of the depth of your involvement at work. Did you supervise others? How many? Did your efforts result in a more efficient operation? How much did you increase efficiency? Did you handle a budget? How much? Were you promoted in a short time? Did you work two jobs at once or fifteen hours per week after high school? Where appropriate, quantify.

Should the Work Section Always Follow the Education Section on the Résumé?
Always lead with your strengths. If your education closely relates to the employment you now seek, put this section after the objective. If your edu-

cation does not closely relate but you have a surplus of good work experiences, consider reversing the order of your sections to lead with employment, followed by education.

How Should I Present My Activities, Honors, Awards, Professional Societies, and Affiliations?

This section of the résumé can add valuable information for an employer to consider if used correctly. The rule of thumb for information in this section is to include only those activities that are in some way relevant to the objective stated on your résumé. If you can draw a valid connection between your activities and your objective, include them; if not, leave them out.

Professional affiliations and honors should all be listed; especially important are those related to your job objective. Social clubs and activities need not be a part of your résumé unless you hold a significant office or you are looking for a position related to your membership. Be aware that most prospective employers' principal concerns are related to your employability, not your social life. If you have any, publications can be included as an addendum to your résumé.

How Should I Handle References?

The use of references is considered a part of the interview process, and they should never be listed on a résumé. You would always provide references to a potential employer if requested to, so it is not even necessary to include this section on the résumé if space does not permit. If space is available, it is acceptable to include the following statement:

- References furnished upon request.

The Functional Résumé

A functional résumé departs from a chronological résumé in that it organizes information by specific accomplishments in various settings: previous jobs, volunteer work, associations, and so forth. This type of résumé permits you to stress the substance of your experiences rather than the position titles you have held. You should consider using a functional résumé if you have held a series of similar jobs that relied on the same skills or abilities. There are many good books in which you can find examples of functional résumés, including *How to Write a Winning Resume* or *Resumes Made Easy*.

The Targeted Résumé

The targeted résumé focuses on specific work-related capabilities you can bring to a given position within an organization. Past achievements are listed to highlight your capabilities and the work history section is abbreviated.

Digital Résumés

Today's employers have to manage an enormous number of résumés. One of the most frequent complaints the writers of this series hear from students is the failure of employers to even acknowledge the receipt of a résumé and cover letter. Frequently, the reason for this poor response or nonresponse is the volume of applications received for every job. In an attempt to better manage the considerable labor investment involved in processing large numbers of résumés, many employers are requiring digital submission of résumés. There are two types of digital résumés: those that can be e-mailed or posted to a website, called *electronic résumés,* and those that can be "read" by a computer, commonly called *scannable résumés.* Though the format may be a bit different from the traditional "paper" résumé, the goal of both types of digital résumés is the same—to get you an interview! These résumés must be designed to be "technologically friendly." What that basically means to you is that they should be free of graphics and fancy formatting. (See Exhibit 2.2.)

Electronic Résumés

Sometimes referred to as plain-text résumés, electronic résumés are designed to be e-mailed to an employer or posted to one of many commercial Internet databases such as Careerbuilder.com, America's Job Bank (ajb.dni.us), or Monster.com.

Some technical considerations:

- Electronic résumés must be written in American Standard Code for Information Interchange (ASCII), which is simply a plain-text format. These characters are universally recognized so that every computer can accurately read and understand them. To create an ASCII file of your current résumé, open your document, then save it as a text or ASCII file. This will eliminate all formatting. Edit as needed using your computer's text editor application.
- Use a standard-width typeface. Courier is a good choice because it is the font associated with ASCII in most systems.

Exhibit 2.2
DIGITAL RÉSUMÉ

JAMEEL CLEVELAND ◄──────────────── Put your name at the
18B Fairview Circle   top on its own line.
Fargo, ND 58107
701-555-6435 (mobile) ◄─────────────── Put your phone number
701-555-7734 (fax)   on its own line.
jaycee17@xxx.com

KEYWORD SUMMARY
B.A. Sociology
Minor: Marketing
Fluent in English, Spanish   Keywords make your
MS Office, Microsoft Word ◄─────────── résumé easier to find in
Research experience   a database.
Marketing research internship
Writing/editing experience

EDUCATION
Bachelor of Arts, Sociology, 2008
University of North Carolina
Minor: Marketing   Use a standard-width
GPA: 3.7/4.0   typeface.

Related Courses
International Marketing
Economics
Marketing Concepts
Statistics
Public Relations
Computer Applications in Business
                                       Capitalize letters to
                                       emphasize heading
COMPUTER SKILLS ◄──────────────────
Word processing
Spreadsheets
Desktop publishing

continued

LANGUAGE SKILLS
Written and spoken Spanish
Written and spoken English
Interpreting experience

No line should exceed sixty-five characters.

EXPERIENCE
Intern, Fargo Chamber of Commerce, Summer 2008:
    Wrote and designed newsletters, maintained files,
    organized meetings

Web Services Specialist, Fike Financial Services,
    Minot, North Dakota, Summer 2007: Responded to
    online requests for assistance, assisted webmaster
    in redesigning site, developed customer tracking
    capabilities

Volunteer activities coordinator, Anderson Senior
    Center, Fargo, North Dakota, Summer 2006:
    Developed social activities for residents, supervised
    four-person volunteer team, planned master activities
    schedule

End each line by hitting the ENTER (or RETURN) key.

COMMUNICATION SKILLS
Highly skilled in written and oral communications
Completed four communication courses
Adept in use of presentation and word-processing
    software

REFERENCES
Available on request
++ Willing to relocate ++

- Use a font size of 11 to 14 points. A 12-point font is considered standard.
- Your margin should be left-justified.
- Do not exceed sixty-five characters per line because the word-wrap function doesn't operate in ASCII.
- Do not use boldface, italics, underlining, bullets, or various font sizes. Instead, use asterisks, plus signs, or all capital letters when you want to emphasize something.

- Avoid graphics and shading.
- Use as many "keywords" as you possibly can. These are words or phrases usually relating to skills or experience that either are specifically used in the job announcement or are popular buzzwords in the industry.
- Minimize abbreviations.
- Your name should be the first line of text.
- Conduct a "test run" by e-mailing your résumé to yourself and a friend before you send it to the employer. See how it transmits, and make any changes you need to. Continue to test it until it's exactly how you want it to look.
- Unless an employer specifically requests that you send the résumé in the form of an attachment, don't. Employers can encounter problems opening a document as an attachment, and there are always viruses to consider.
- Don't forget your cover letter. Send it along with your résumé as a single message.

Scannable Résumés

Some companies are relying on technology to narrow the candidate pool for available job openings. Electronic Applicant Tracking uses imaging to scan, sort, and store résumé elements in a database. Then, through OCR (Optical Character Recognition) software, the computer scans the résumés for keywords and phrases. To have the best chance at getting an interview, you want to increase the number of "hits"—matches of your skills, abilities, experience, and education to those the computer is scanning for—your résumé will get. You can see how critical using the right keywords is for this type of résumé.

Technical considerations include:

- Again, do not use boldface (newer systems may be able to read this, but many older ones won't), italics, underlining, bullets, shading, graphics, or multiple font sizes. Instead, for emphasis, use asterisks, plus signs, or all capital letters. Minimize abbreviations.
- Use a popular typeface such as Courier, Helvetica, Arial, or Palatino. Avoid decorative fonts.
- Font size should be between 11 and 14 points.
- Do not compress the spacing between letters.
- Use horizontal and vertical lines sparingly; the computer may misread them as the letters *L* or *I*.

- Left-justify the text.
- Do not use parentheses or brackets around telephone numbers, and be sure your phone number is on its own line of text.
- Your name should be the first line of text and on its own line. If your résumé is longer than one page, be sure to put your name on the top of all pages.
- Use a traditional résumé structure. The chronological format may work best.
- Use nouns that are skill-focused, such as *management, writer,* and *programming.* This is different from traditional paper résumés, which use action-oriented verbs.
- Laser printers produce the finest copies. Avoid dot-matrix printers.
- Use standard, light-colored paper with text on one side only. Since the higher the contrast, the better, your best choice is black ink on white paper.
- Always send original copies. If you must fax, set the fax on fine mode, not standard.
- Do not staple or fold your résumé. This can confuse the computer.
- Before you send your scannable résumé, be certain the employer uses this technology. If you can't determine this, you may want to send two versions (scannable and traditional) to be sure your résumé gets considered.

Résumé Production and Other Tips

An ink-jet printer is the preferred option for printing your résumé. Begin by printing just a few copies. You may find a small error or you may simply want to make some changes, and it is less frustrating and less expensive if you print in small batches.

Résumé paper color should be carefully chosen. You should consider the types of employers who will receive your résumé and the types of positions for which you are applying. Use white or ivory paper for traditional or conservative employers or for higher-level positions.

Black ink on sharp, white paper can be harsh on the reader's eyes. Think about an ivory or cream paper that will provide less contrast and be easier to read. Pink, green, and blue tints should generally be avoided.

Many résumé writers buy packages of matching envelopes and cover sheet stationery that, although not absolutely necessary, help convey a professional impression.

If you'll be producing many cover letters at home, be sure you have high-quality printing equipment. Learn standard envelope formats for business, and retain a copy of every cover letter you send out. You can use the copies to take notes of any telephone conversations that may occur.

If attending a job fair, either carry a briefcase or place your résumé in a nicely covered legal-size pad holder.

The Cover Letter

The cover letter provides you with the opportunity to tailor your résumé by telling the prospective employer how you can be a benefit to the organization. It allows you to highlight aspects of your background that are not already discussed in your résumé and that might be especially relevant to the organization you are contacting or to the position you are seeking. Every résumé should have a cover letter enclosed when you send it out. Unlike the résumé, which may be mass-produced, a cover letter is most effective when it is individually prepared and focused on the particular requirements of the organization in question.

A good cover letter should supplement the résumé and motivate the reader to review the résumé. The format shown in Exhibit 2.3 (see page 35) is only a suggestion to help you decide what information to include in a cover letter.

Begin the cover letter with your street address six lines down from the top. Leave three to five lines between the date and the name of the person to whom you are addressing the cover letter. Make sure you leave one blank line between the salutation and the body of the letter and between paragraphs. After typing "Sincerely," leave four blank lines and type your name. This should leave plenty of room for your signature. A sample cover letter is shown in Exhibit 2.4 on page 36.

The following guidelines will help you write good cover letters:

1. Be sure to type your letter neatly; ensure there are no misspellings.
2. Avoid unusual typefaces, such as script.
3. Address the letter to an individual, using the person's name and title. To obtain this information, call the company. If answering a blind newspaper advertisement, address the letter "To Whom It May Concern" or omit the salutation.
4. Be sure your cover letter directly indicates the position you are applying for and tells why you are qualified to fill it.

5. Send the original letter, not a photocopy, with your résumé. Keep a copy for your records.
6. Make your cover letter no more than one page.
7. Include a phone number where you can be reached.
8. Avoid trite language and have someone read the letter over to react to its tone, content, and mechanics.
9. For your own information, record the date you send out each letter and résumé.

Exhibit 2.3
COVER LETTER FORMAT

Your Street Address
Your Town, State, Zip
Phone Number
Fax Number
Date   E-mail

Name
Title
Organization
Address

Dear _____:

First Paragraph. In this paragraph state the reason for the letter, name the specific position or type of work you are applying for, and indicate from which resource (career services office, website, newspaper, contact, employment service) you learned of this opening. The first paragraph can also be used to inquire about future openings.

Second Paragraph. Indicate why you are interested in this position, the company, or its products or services and what you can do for the employer. If you are a recent graduate, explain how your academic background makes you a qualified candidate. Try not to repeat the same information found in the résumé.

Third Paragraph. Refer the reader to the enclosed résumé for more detailed information.

Fourth Paragraph. In this paragraph say what you will do to follow up on your letter. For example, state that you will call by a certain date to set up an interview or to find out if the company will be recruiting in your area. Finish by indicating your willingness to answer any questions the recipient may have. Be sure you have provided your phone number.

Sincerely,

Type your name

Enclosure

Exhibit 2.4
SAMPLE COVER LETTER
_____

Tonya A. Smith
2300 South Gateway
Kansas City, MO 64116
816-555-6367
816-555-4882 (cell)
Tonyasmith@xxx.net

October 12, 2008

Mr. C. W. Adcock
Executive Director
Association of Family Services
2312 DuPont Circle
Washington, DC 20002

Dear Mr. Adcock:

Please accept the enclosed résumé and letters of recommendation in application for the position of assistant program director at your organization. This is in response to the job vacancy notice published this week in the *Washington Post*.

As you will gather from my résumé, I have a solid knowledge of the issues facing today's families through my studies at Lipscomb College and Kansas State University, as well as my experiences working for two social service organizations. In addition, my two years of experience with the Midwest Association of Family Services has entailed responsibilities that are very similar to those outlined in your position description. In fact, I believe that my professional and educational background provide the ideal qualifications you are seeking.

I have always had a strong interest promoting family growth and development, and I would enjoy the opportunity to apply my experience to the challenges of an organization such as yours. I would appreciate an interview at your convenience. I can be reached at 816-555-4882 at any time through my voice mail service.

Thank you for your consideration. I look forward to your response.

Sincerely,

Tonya A. Smith

Enclosure

3

Researching Careers and Networking

What do they call the job you want? One reason for confusion is perhaps a mistaken assumption that a college education provides job training. In most cases it does not. Of course, applied fields such as engineering, management, or education provide specific skills for the workplace as well as an education. Regardless, your overall college education exposes you to numerous fields of study and teaches you quantitative reasoning, critical thinking, writing, and speaking, all of which can be successfully applied to a number of different job fields. But it still remains up to you to choose a job field and to learn how to articulate the benefits of your education in a way the employer will appreciate.

The sociology major covers a more broad-based spectrum of activity than you might realize. In fact, you'll find sociology majors employed in every sector of the economy. This includes not only the corporate world but also government, academia, and the non-profit sector.

Collect Job Titles

The world of employment is a complex place, so you need to become a bit of an explorer and adventurer and be willing to try a variety of techniques to develop a list of possible occupations that might use your talents and education. You might find computerized interest inventories, reference books and other sources, and classified ads helpful in this respect. Once you have a list of possibilities that you are interested in and qualified for, you can move on to find out what kinds of organizations have these job titles.

Computerized Interest Inventories

One way to begin collecting job titles is to identify a number of jobs that call for your degree and the particular skills and interests you identified as part of the self-assessment process. There are excellent interactive career-guidance programs on the market to help you produce such selected lists of possible job titles. Most of these are available at colleges and at some larger town and city libraries. Two of the industry leaders are *CHOICES* and *DIS-COVER*. Both allow you to enter interests, values, educational background, and other information to produce lists of possible occupations and industries. Each of the resources listed here will produce different job title lists. Some job titles will appear again and again, while others will be unique to a particular source. Investigate all of them!

Reference Sources

Books on the market that may be available through your local library or career counseling office also suggest various occupations related to specific majors. The following are only a few of the many good books on the market: *The College Board Guide to 150 College Majors* and *College Majors and Careers: A Resource Guide for Effective Life Planning* both by Paul Phifer, and *Kaplan's What to Study: 101 Fields in a Flash*. All of these books list possible job titles within the academic major.

Some employment environments may be more attractive to you than others. If you are considering a career in public relations research, you might pursue that option as a staff member at a marketing research firm, a member of the research and development or marketing department at a large corporation, a research specialist with a government agency, or a staff member at a nonprofit social service organization. Although these jobs might involve similar skills, each environment presents a different culture with associated norms in the pace of work, the interaction with others, and the background and training of those you'll work with or encounter on the job. Even in roles where job titles are quite similar, not all situations will present the same "fit" for you.

If you majored in sociology and enjoyed writing, doing research, and making in-class presentations, and along the way you developed both mastery of the subject matter and some strong oral communication and presentation skills, you might think of a postsecondary teaching career. But sociology majors with some of these same skills and interests go on to work as analysts, human resource specialists, social workers, and employees or managers in nonprofit organizations, among other possibilities. In some cases, additional education or training might be required. Each job title within the overall list of sociology career positions can be found in a variety of settings.

Each job title deserves your consideration. Like removing the layers of an onion, the search for job titles can go on and on! As you spend time doing this activity, you are actually learning more about the value of your degree. What's important in your search at this point is not to become critical or selective but rather to develop as long a list of possibilities as you can. Every source used will help you add new and potentially exciting jobs to your growing list.

Classified Ads

It has been well publicized that the classified ad section of the newspaper represents only a small fraction of the current job market. Nevertheless, the weekly classified ads can be a great help to you in your search. Although they may not be the best place to look for a job, they can teach you a lot about the job market. Classified ads provide a good education in job descriptions, duties, responsibilities, and qualifications. In addition, they provide insight into which industries are actively recruiting and some indication of the area's employment market. This is particularly helpful when seeking a position in a specific geographic area and/or a specific field. For your purposes, classified ads are a good source for job titles to add to your list.

Read the Sunday classified ads in a major market newspaper for several weeks in a row. Cut and paste all the ads that interest you and seem to call for something close to your education, skills, experience, and interests. Remember that classified ads are written for what an organization *hopes* to find; you don't have to meet absolutely every criterion. However, if certain requirements are stated as absolute minimums and you cannot meet them, it's best not to waste your time and that of the employer.

The weekly classified want ads exercise is important because these jobs are out in the marketplace. They truly exist, and people with your qualifications are being sought to apply. What's more, many of these advertisements describe the duties and responsibilities of the job advertised and give you a beginning sense of the challenges and opportunities such a position presents. Some will indicate salary, and that will be helpful as well. This information will better define the jobs for you and provide some good material for possible interviews in that field.

Explore Job Descriptions

Once you've arrived at a solid list of possible job titles that interest you and for which you believe you are somewhat qualified, it's a good idea to do some research on each of these jobs. The preeminent source for such job information is the *Dictionary of Occupational Titles*, or *DOT* (wave.net/upg/ immigration/dot_index.html). This directory lists every conceivable job and provides excellent up-to-date information on duties and responsibilities, interactions with associates, and day-to-day assignments and tasks. These descriptions provide a thorough job analysis, but they do not consider the possible employers or the environments in which a job may be performed. So, although a position as public relations officer may be well defined in terms of duties and responsibilities, it does not explain the differences in doing public relations work in a college or a hospital or a factory or a bank. You will need to look somewhere else for work settings.

Learn More About Possible Work Settings

After reading some job descriptions, you may choose to edit and revise your list of job titles once again, discarding those you feel are not suitable and keeping those that continue to hold your interest. Or you may wish to keep your list intact and see where these jobs may be located. For example, if you are interested in public relations and you appear to have those skills and the requisite education, you'll want to know which organizations do public relations. How can you find that out? How much income does someone in public relations make a year and what is the employment potential for the field of public relations?

To answer these and many other questions about your list of job titles, we recommend you try any of the following resources: *Careers Encyclopedia*, the professional societies and resources found throughout this book, *College to Career: The Guide to Job Opportunities*, and the *Occupational Outlook Handbook* (http://stats.bls.gov/ocohome.htm). Each of these resources, in a different way, will help to put the job titles you have selected into an employer context. Perhaps the most extensive discussion is found in the *Occupational Outlook Handbook*, which gives a thorough presentation of the nature of the work, the working conditions, employment statistics, training, other qualifications, and advancement possibilities as well as job outlook and earnings. Related occupations are also detailed, and a select bibliography is provided to help you find additional information.

Continuing with our public relations example, your search through these reference materials would teach you that the public relations jobs you find attractive are available in larger hospitals, financial institutions, most corporations (both consumer goods and industrial goods), media organizations, and colleges and universities.

Networking

Networking is the process of deliberately establishing relationships to get career-related information or to alert potential employers that you are available for work. Networking is critically important to today's job seeker for two reasons: it will help you get the information you need, and it can help you find out about *all* of the available jobs.

Get the Information You Need

Networkers will review your résumé and give you feedback on its effectiveness. They will talk about the job you are looking for and give you a candid appraisal of how they see your strengths and weaknesses. If they have a good sense of the industry or the employment sector for that job, you'll get their feelings on future trends in the industry as well. Some networkers will be very forthcoming about salaries, job-hunting techniques, and suggestions for your job search strategy. Many have been known to place calls right from the interview desk to friends and associates who might be interested in you. Each networker will make his or her own contribution, and each will be valuable.

Because organizations must evolve to adapt to current global market needs, the information provided by decision makers within various organizations will be critical to your success as a new job market entrant. For example, you might learn about the concept of virtual organizations from a networker. Virtual organizations coordinate economic activity to deliver value to customers by using resources outside the traditional boundaries of the organization. This concept is being discussed and implemented by chief executive officers of many organizations, including Ford Motor, Dell, and IBM. Networking can help you find out about this and other trends currently affecting the industries under your consideration.

Find Out About All of the Available Jobs

Not every job that is available at this very moment is advertised for potential applicants to see. This is called the *hidden job market*. Only 15 to 20 percent of all jobs are formally advertised, which means that 80 to 85 percent of available jobs do not appear in published channels. Networking will help you become more knowledgeable about all the employment opportunities available during your job search period.

Although someone you might talk to today doesn't know of any openings within his or her organization, tomorrow or next week or next month an opening may occur. If you've taken the time to show an interest in and knowledge of their organization, if you've shown the company representative how you can help achieve organizational goals and that you can fit into the organization, you'll be one of the first candidates considered for the position.

Networking: A Proactive Approach

Networking is a proactive rather than a reactive approach. You, as a job seeker, are expected to initiate a certain level of activity on your own behalf; you cannot afford to simply respond to jobs listed in the newspaper. Being proactive means building a network of contacts that includes informed and interested decision makers who will provide you with up-to-date knowledge of the current job market and increase your chances of finding out about employment opportunities appropriate for your interests, experience, and level of education. An old axiom of networking says, "You are only two phone calls away from the information you need." In other words, by talking to enough people, you will quickly come across someone who can offer you help.

Preparing to Network

In deliberately establishing relationships, maximize your efforts by organizing your approach. Five specific areas in which you can organize your efforts include reviewing your self-assessment, reviewing your research on job sites and organizations, deciding who you want to talk to, keeping track of all your efforts, and creating your self-promotion tools.

Review Your Self-Assessment

Your self-assessment is as important a tool in preparing to network as it has been in other aspects of your job search. You have carefully evaluated your personal traits, personal values, economic needs, longer-term goals, skill base, preferred skills, and underdeveloped skills. During the networking process you will be called upon to communicate what you know about yourself and relate it to the information or job you seek. Be sure to review the exercises that you completed in the self-assessment section of this book in preparation for networking. We've explained that you need to assess which skills you have acquired from your major that are of general value to an employer; be ready to express those in ways he or she can appreciate as useful in the organizations.

Review Research on Job Sites and Organizations

In addition, individuals assisting you will expect that you'll have at least some background information on the occupation or industry of interest to you. Refer to the appropriate sections of this book and other relevant publications to acquire the background information necessary for effective networking. They'll explain how to identify not only the job titles that might be of interest to you but also which kinds of organizations employ people to do that job. You will develop some sense of working conditions and expectations about duties and responsibilities—all of which will be of help in your networking interviews.

Decide Whom You Want to Talk To

Networking cannot begin until you decide whom you want to talk to and, in general, what type of information you hope to gain from your contacts. Once you know this, it's time to begin developing a list of contacts. Five useful sources for locating contacts are described here.

College Alumni Network. Most colleges and universities have created a formal network of alumni and friends of the institution who are particularly interested in helping currently enrolled students and graduates of their alma mater gain employment-related information.

It is usually a simple process to make use of an alumni network. Visit your college's website and locate the alumni office and/or your career center.

Either or both sites will have information about your school's alumni network. You'll be provided with information on shadowing experiences, geographic information, or those alumni offering job referrals. If you don't find what you're looking for, don't hesitate to phone or e-mail your career center and ask what they can do to help you connect with an alum.

Alumni networkers may provide some combination of the following services: day-long shadowing experiences, telephone interviews, in-person interviews, information on relocating to given geographic areas, internship information, suggestions on graduate school study, and job vacancy notices.

Present and Former Supervisors. If you believe you are on good terms with present or former job supervisors, they may be an excellent resource for providing information or directing you to appropriate resources that would have information related to your current interests and needs. Additionally, these supervisors probably belong to professional organizations that they might be willing to utilize to get information for you.

Employers in Your Area. Although you may be interested in working in a geographic location different from the one where you currently reside, don't overlook the value of the knowledge and contacts those around you are able to provide. Use the local telephone directory and newspaper to identify the types of organizations you are thinking of working for or professionals who have the kinds of jobs you are interested in. Recently, a call made to a local hospital's financial administrator for information on working in health-care financial administration yielded more pertinent information on training seminars, regional professional organizations, and potential employment sites than a national organization was willing to provide.

Employers in Geographic Areas Where You Hope to Work. If you are thinking about relocating, identifying prospective employers or informational contacts in the new location will be critical to your success. Here are some tips for online searching. First, use a "metasearch" engine to get the most out of your search. Metasearch engines combine several engines into one powerful tool. We frequently use dogpile.com and metasearch.com for this purpose. Try using the city and state as your keywords in a search. *New Haven, Connecticut* will bring you to the city's website with links to the chamber of commerce, member businesses, and other valuable resources. By using looksmart.com you can locate newspapers in any area, and they, too, can provide valuable insight before you relocate. Of course, both dogpile and metasearch can lead you to yellow and white page directories in areas you are considering.

Professional Associations and Organizations. Professional associations and organizations can provide valuable information in several areas: career paths that you might not have considered, qualifications relating to those career choices, publications that list current job openings, and workshops or seminars that will enhance your professional knowledge and skills. They can also be excellent sources for background information on given industries: their health, current problems, and future challenges.

There are several excellent resources available to help you locate professional associations and organizations that would have information to meet your needs. Two especially useful publications are the *Encyclopedia of Associations* and *National Trade and Professional Associations of the United States.*

Keep Track of All Your Efforts

It can be difficult, almost impossible, to remember all the details related to each contact you make during the networking process, so you will want to develop a record-keeping system that works for you. Formalize this process by using your computer to keep a record of the people and organizations you want to contact. You can simply record the contact's name, address, and telephone number, and what information you hope to gain.

You could record this as a simple Word document and you could still use the "Find" function if you were trying to locate some data and could only recall the firm's name or the contact's name. If you're comfortable with database management and you have some database software on your computer, then you can put information at your fingertips even if you have only the zip code! The point here is not technological sophistication but good record keeping.

Once you have created this initial list, it will be helpful to keep more detailed information as you begin to actually make the contacts. Those details should include complete contact information, the date and content of each contact, names and information for additional networkers, and required follow-up. Don't forget to send a letter thanking your contact for his or her time! Your contact will appreciate your recall of details of your meetings and conversations, and the information will help you to focus your networking efforts.

Create Your Self-Promotion Tools

There are two types of promotional tools that are used in the networking process. The first is a résumé and cover letter, and the second is a one-minute "infomercial," which may be given over the telephone or in person.

Techniques for writing an effective résumé and cover letter are discussed in Chapter 2. Once you have reviewed that material and prepared these important documents, you will have created one of your self-promotion tools.

The one-minute infomercial will demand that you begin tying your interests, abilities, and skills to the people or organizations you want to network with. Think about your goal for making the contact to help you understand what you should say about yourself. You should be able to express yourself easily and convincingly. If, for example, you are contacting an alumnus of your institution to obtain the names of possible employment sites in a distant city, be prepared to discuss why you are interested in moving to that location, the types of jobs you are interested in, and the skills and abilities you possess that will make you a qualified candidate.

To create a meaningful one-minute infomercial, write it out, practice it as if it will be a spoken presentation, rewrite it, and practice it again if necessary until expressing yourself comes easily and is convincing.

Here's a simplified example of an infomercial for use over the telephone:

Hello, Mr. Chandler? My name is Allison Liao. I am a recent graduate of Michigan State University, and I wish to enter the field of marketing research. I feel confident I have many of the skills I understand are valued for professionals in this area. Along with a degree in sociology and a minor in business, I have a strong quantitative background, with good research and computer skills. In addition, I have excellent interpersonal skills and am known as a creative thinker. I understand these are valuable traits in your line of work!

Mr. Chandler, I'm calling you because I still need more information about marketing as a profession and where I might fit in. I'm hoping you'll have time to sit down with me for about half an hour to discuss your perspective on careers in marketing with me. There are so many possible employers to approach, and I am seeking some advice on which might be the best bet for my particular combination of skills and experience.

Would you be willing to do that for me? I would greatly appreciate it. I am available most mornings, if that's convenient for you.

It very well may happen that your employer contact wishes you to communicate by e-mail. The infomercial quoted above could easily be rewritten for an e-mail message. You should "cut and paste" your résumé right into the e-mail text itself.

Other effective self-promotion tools include portfolios for those in the arts, writing professions, or teaching. Portfolios show examples of work, photographs of projects or classroom activities, or certificates and credentials that are job related. There may not be an opportunity to use the portfolio during an interview, and it is not something that should be left with the organization. It is designed to be explained and displayed by the creator. However, during some networking meetings, there may be an opportunity to illustrate a point or strengthen a qualification by exhibiting the portfolio.

Beginning the Networking Process

Set the Tone for Your Communications
It can be useful to establish "tone words" for any communications you embark upon. Before making your first telephone call or writing your first letter, decide what you want the person to think of you. If you are networking to try to obtain a job, your tone words might include descriptors such as *genuine*, *informed*, and *self-knowledgeable*. When you're trying to acquire information, your tone words may have a slightly different focus, such as *courteous*, *organized*, *focused*, and *well-spoken*. Use the tone words you establish for your contacts to guide you through the networking process.

Honestly Express Your Intentions
When contacting individuals, it is important to be honest about your reasons for making the contact. Establish your purpose in your own mind and be able and ready to articulate it concisely. Determine an initial agenda, whether it be informational questioning or self-promotion, present it to your contact, and be ready to respond immediately. If you don't adequately prepare before initiating your overture, you may find yourself at a disadvantage if you're asked to immediately begin your informational interview or self-promotion during the first phone conversation or visit.

Start Networking Within Your Circle of Confidence
Once you have organized your approach—by utilizing specific researching methods, creating a system for keeping track of the people you will contact, and developing effective self-promotion tools—you are ready to begin networking. The best way to begin networking is by talking with a group of people you trust and feel comfortable with. This group is usually made up

of your family, friends, and career counselors. No matter who is in this inner circle, they will have a special interest in seeing you succeed in your job search. In addition, because they will be easy to talk to, you should try taking some risks in terms of practicing your information-seeking approach. Gain confidence in talking about the strengths you bring to an organization and the underdeveloped skills you feel hinder your candidacy. Be sure to review the section on self-assessment for tips on approaching each of these areas. Ask for critical but constructive feedback from the people in your circle of confidence on the letters you write and the one-minute infomercial you have developed. Evaluate whether you want to make the changes they suggest, then practice the changes on others within this circle.

Stretch the Boundaries of Your Networking Circle of Confidence

Once you have refined the promotional tools you will use to accomplish your networking goals, you will want to make additional contacts. Because you will not know most of these people, it will be a less comfortable activity to undertake. The practice that you gained with your inner circle of trusted friends should have prepared you to now move outside of that comfort zone.

It is said that any information a person needs is only two phone calls away, but the information cannot be gained until you (1) make a reasonable guess about who might have the information you need and (2) pick up the telephone to make the call. Using your network list that includes alumni, instructors, supervisors, employers, and associations, you can begin preparing your list of questions that will allow you to get the information you need.

Prepare the Questions You Want to Ask

Networkers can provide you with the insider's perspective on any given field and you can ask them questions that you might not want to ask in an interview. For example, you can ask them to describe the more repetitious or mundane parts of the job or ask them for a realistic idea of salary expectations. Be sure to prepare your questions ahead of time so that you are organized and efficient.

Be Prepared to Answer Some Questions

To communicate effectively, you must anticipate questions that will be asked of you by the networkers you contact. Revisit the self-assessment process you undertook and the research you've done so that you can effortlessly respond to questions about your short- and long-term goals and the kinds of jobs you are most interested in pursuing.

General Networking Tips

Make Every Contact Count. Setting the tone for each interaction is critical. Approaches that will help you communicate in an effective way include politeness, being appreciative of time provided to you, and being prepared and thorough. Remember, *everyone* within an organization has a circle of influence, so be prepared to interact effectively with each person you encounter in the networking process, including secretarial and support staff. Many information or job seekers have thwarted their own efforts by being rude to some individuals they encountered as they networked because they made the incorrect assumption that certain persons were unimportant.

Sometimes your contacts may be surprised at their ability to help you. After meeting and talking with you, they might think they have not offered much in the way of help. A day or two later, however, they may make a contact that would be useful to you and refer you to that person.

With Each Contact, Widen Your Circle of Networkers. Always leave an informational interview with the names of at least two more people who can help you get the information or job that you are seeking. Don't be shy about asking for additional contacts; networking is all about increasing the number of people you can interact with to achieve your goals.

Make Your Own Decisions. As you talk with different people and get answers to the questions you pose, you may hear conflicting information or get conflicting suggestions. Your job is to listen to these "experts" and decide what information and which suggestions will help you achieve *your* goals. Only implement those suggestions that you believe will work for you.

Shutting Down Your Network

As you achieve the goals that motivated your networking activity—getting the information you need or the job you want—the time will come to inactivate all or parts of your network. As you do, be sure to tell your primary supporters about your change in status. Call or write to each one of them and give them as many details about your new status as you feel is necessary to maintain a positive relationship.

Because a network takes on a life of its own, activity undertaken on your behalf will continue even after you cease your efforts. As you get calls or are contacted in some fashion, be sure to inform these networkers about your change in status, and thank them for assistance they have provided.

Information on the latest employment trends indicates that workers will change jobs or careers several times in their lifetime. Networking, then, will be a critical aspect in the span of your professional life. If you carefully and thoughtfully conduct your networking activities during your job search, you will have a solid foundation of experience when you need to network the next time around.

Where Are These Jobs, Anyway?

Having a list of job titles that you've designed around your own career interests and skills is an excellent beginning. It means you've really thought about who you are and what you are presenting to the employment market. It has caused you to think seriously about the most appealing environments to work in, and you have identified some employer types that represent these environments.

The research and the thinking that you've done thus far will be used again and again. They will be helpful in writing your résumé and cover letters, in talking about yourself on the telephone to prospective employers, and in answering interview questions.

Now is a good time to begin to narrow the field of job titles and employment sites down to some specific employers to initiate the employment contact.

Find Out Which Employers Hire People Like You

This section will provide tips, techniques, and specific resources for developing an actual list of specific employers that can be used to make contacts. It is only an outline that you must be prepared to tailor to your own particular needs and according to what you bring to the job search. Once again, it is important to communicate with others along the way exactly what you're looking for and what your goals are for the research you're doing. Librarians, employers, career counselors, friends, friends of friends, business contacts, and bookstore staff will all have helpful information on geographically specific and new resources to aid you in locating employers who'll hire you.

Identify Information Resources

Your interview wardrobe and your new résumé might have put a dent in your wallet, but the resources you'll need to pursue your job search are available for free. The categories of information detailed here are not hard to find and are yours for the browsing.

Numerous resources described in this section will help you identify actual employers. Use all of them or any others that you identify as available in your geographic area. As you become experienced in this process, you'll quickly figure out which information sources are helpful and which are not. If you live in a rural area, a well-planned day trip to a major city that includes a college career office, a large college or city library, state and federal employment centers, a chamber of commerce office, and a well-stocked bookstore can produce valuable results.

There are many excellent resources available to help you identify actual job sites. They are categorized into employer directories (usually indexed by product lines and geographic location), geographically based directories (designed to highlight particular cities, regions, or states), career-specific directories (e.g., *Sports MarketPlace*, which lists tens of thousands of firms involved with sports), periodicals and newspapers, targeted job posting publications, and videos. This is by no means meant to be a complete treatment of resources but rather a starting point for identifying useful resources.

Working from the more general references to highly specific resources, we provide a basic list to help you begin your search. Many of these you'll find easily available. In some cases reference librarians and others will suggest even better materials for your particular situation. Start to create your own customized bibliography of job search references.

Geographically Based Directories. The Job Bank series published by Bob Adams, Inc. (aip.com) contains detailed entries on each area's major employers, including business activity, address, phone number, and hiring contact name. Many listings specify educational backgrounds being sought in potential employees. Each volume contains a solid discussion of each city's or state's major employment sectors. Organizations are also indexed by industry. Job Bank volumes are available for the following places: Atlanta, Boston, Chicago, Dallas–Ft. Worth, Denver, Detroit, Florida, Houston, Los Angeles, Minneapolis, New York, Ohio, Philadelphia, San Francisco, Seattle, St. Louis, Washington, D.C., and other cities throughout the Northwest.

National Job Bank (careercity.com) lists employers in every state, along with contact names and commonly hired job categories. Included are many small companies often overlooked by other directories. Companies are also indexed by industry. This publication provides information on educational backgrounds sought and lists company benefits.

Periodicals and Newspapers. Several sources are available to help you locate which journals or magazines carry job advertisements in your field. Other resources help you identify opportunities in other parts of the country.

- *Where the Jobs Are: A Comprehensive Directory of 1200 Journals Listing Career Opportunities*
- *Corptech Fast 5000 Company Locator*
- *National Ad Search* (nationaladsearch.com)
- *The Federal Jobs Digest* (jobsfed.com) and *Federal Career Opportunities*
- *World Chamber of Commerce Directory* (chamberofcommerce.org)

This list is certainly not exhaustive; use it to begin your job search work.

Targeted Job Posting Publications. Although the resources that follow are national in scope, they are either targeted to one medium of contact (telephone), focused on specific types of jobs, or less comprehensive than the sources previously listed.

- Careers.org (careers.org/index.html)
- *The Job Hunter* (jobhunter.com)
- *Current Jobs for Graduates* (graduatejobs.com)
- *Environmental Opportunities* (ecojobs.com)
- *Y National Vacancy List* (ymca.net/employment/ymca_recruiting/jobright.htm)
- *ArtSEARCH*
- *Community Jobs*
- *National Association of Colleges and Employers: Job Choices series*
- *National Association of Colleges and Employers* (jobweb.com)

Videos. You may be one of the many job seekers who likes to get information via a medium other than paper. Many career libraries, public libraries, and career centers in libraries carry an assortment of videos that will help you learn new techniques and get information helpful in the job search.

Locate Information Resources

Throughout these introductory chapters, we have continually referred you to various websites for information on everything from job listings to career information. Using the Web gives you a mobility at your computer that you don't enjoy if you rely solely on books or newspapers or printed journals. Moreover, material on the Web, if the site is maintained, can be the most up-to-date information available.

You'll eventually identify the information resources that work best for you, but make certain you've covered the full range of resources before you begin to rely on a smaller list. Here's a short list of informational sites that many job seekers find helpful:

- Public and college libraries
- College career centers
- Bookstores
- The Internet
- Local and state government personnel offices
- Career/job fairs

Each one of these sites offers a collection of resources that will help you get the information you need.

As you meet and talk with service professionals at all these sites, be sure to let them know what you're doing. Inform them of your job search, what you've already accomplished, and what you're looking for. The more people who know you're job seeking, the greater the possibility that someone will have information or know someone who can help you along your way.

4

Interviewing and Job Offer Considerations

Certainly, there can be no one part of the job search process more fraught with anxiety and worry than the interview. Yet seasoned job seekers welcome the interview and will often say, "Just get me an interview and I'm on my way!" They understand that the interview is crucial to the hiring process and equally crucial for them, as job candidates, to have the opportunity of a personal dialogue to add to what the employer may already have learned from the résumé, cover letter, and telephone conversations.

Believe it or not, the interview is to be welcomed, and even enjoyed! It is a perfect opportunity for you, the candidate, to sit down with an employer and express yourself and display who you are and what you want. Of course, it takes thought and planning and a little strategy; after all, it *is* a job interview! But it can be a positive, if not pleasant, experience and one you can look back on and feel confident about your performance and effort.

For many new job seekers, a job, any job, seems a wonderful thing. But seasoned interview veterans know that the job interview is an important step for both sides—the employer and the candidate—to see what each has to offer and whether there is going to be a "fit" of personalities, work styles, and attitudes. And it is this concept of balance in the interview, that both sides have important parts to play, that holds the key to success in mastering this aspect of the job search strategy.

Try to think of the interview as a conversation between two interested and equal partners. You both have important, even vital, information to deliver and to learn. Of course, there's no denying the employer has some leverage, especially in the initial interview for recruitment or any interview scheduled by the candidate and not the recruiter. That should not prevent the interviewee from seeking to play an equal part in what should be a fair exchange of information. Too often the untutored candidate allows the interview to become one-sided. The employer asks all the questions and the candidate simply responds. The ideal would be for two mutually interested parties to sit down and discuss possibilities for each. This is a conversation of significance, and it requires preparation, thought about the tone of the interview, and planning of the nature and details of the information to be exchanged.

Preparing for the Interview

The length of most initial interviews is about thirty minutes. Given the brevity, the information that is exchanged ought to be important. The candidate should be delivering material that the employer cannot discover on the résumé, and in turn, the candidate should be learning things about the employer that he or she could not otherwise find out. After all, if you have only thirty minutes, why waste time on information that is already published? The information exchanged is more than just factual, and both sides will learn much from what they see of each other, as well. How the candidate looks, speaks, and acts are important to the employer. The employer's attention to the interview and awareness of the candidate's résumé, the setting, and the quality of information presented are important to the candidate.

Just as the employer has every right to be disappointed when a prospect is late for the interview, looks unkempt, and seems ill-prepared to answer fairly standard questions, the candidate may be disappointed with an interviewer who isn't ready for the meeting, hasn't learned the basic résumé facts, and is constantly interrupted by telephone calls. In either situation there's good reason to feel let down.

There are many elements to a successful interview, and some of them are not easy to describe or prepare for. Sometimes there is just a chemistry between interviewer and interviewee that brings out the best in both, and a good exchange takes place. But there is much the candidate can do to pave the way for success in terms of his or her résumé, personal appearance, goals, and interview strategy—each of which we will discuss. However, none of this preparation is as important as the time and thought the candidate gives to personal self-assessment.

Self-Assessment
Neither a stunning résumé nor an expensive, well-tailored suit can compensate for candidates who do not know what they want, where they are going, or why they are interviewing with a particular employer. Self-assessment, the process by which we begin to know and acknowledge our own particular

blend of education, experiences, needs, and goals, is not something that can be sorted out the weekend before a major interview. Of all the elements of interview preparation, this one requires the longest lead time and cannot be faked.

Because the time allotted for most interviews is brief, it is all the more important for job candidates to understand and express succinctly why they are there and what they have to offer. This is not a time for undue modesty (or for braggadocio either); it is a time for a compelling, reasoned statement of why you feel that you and this employer might make a good match. It means you have to have thought about your skills, interests, and attributes; related those to your life experiences and your own history of challenges and opportunities; and determined what that indicates about your strengths, preferences, values, and areas needing further development.

If you need some assistance with self-assessment issues, refer to Chapter 1. Included are suggested exercises that can be done as needed, such as making up an experiential diary and extracting obvious strengths and weaknesses from past experiences. These simple assignments will help you look at past activities as collections of tasks with accompanying skills and responsibilities. Don't overlook your high school or college career office. Many offer personal counseling on self-assessment issues and may provide testing instruments such as the *Myers-Briggs Type Indicator (MBTI)*, the *Harrington-O'Shea Career Decision-Making System (CDM)*, the *Strong Interest Inventory (SII)*, or any other of a wide selection of assessment tools that can help you clarify some of these issues prior to the interview stage of your job search.

The Résumé

Résumé preparation has been discussed in detail, and some basic examples were provided. In this section we want to concentrate on how best to use your résumé in the interview. In most cases the employer will have seen the résumé prior to the interview, and, in fact, it may well have been the quality of that résumé that secured the interview opportunity.

An interview is a conversation, however, and not an exercise in reading. So, if the employer hasn't seen your résumé and you have brought it along to the interview, wait until asked or until the end of the interview to offer it. Otherwise, you may find yourself staring at the back of your résumé and simply answering "yes" and "no" to a series of questions drawn from that document.

Sometimes an interviewer is not prepared and does not know or recall the contents of the résumé and may use the résumé to a greater or lesser degree as a "prompt" during the interview. It is for you to judge what that may indicate about the individual performing the interview or the employer.

If your interviewer seems surprised by the scheduled meeting, relies on the résumé to an inordinate degree, and seems otherwise unfamiliar with your background, this lack of preparation for the hiring process could well be a symptom of general management disorganization or may simply be the result of poor planning on the part of one individual. It is your responsibility as a potential employee to be aware of these signals and make your decisions accordingly.

It is entirely acceptable for you to bring the conversation back to a more interpersonal style by saying something like, "Ms. Huber, you might be interested in some recent experience I gained in a volunteer position at our local women's shelter that is not reflected on my application. May I tell you about this experience?" Such an approach can change the interview from one person reading and another responding to a conversation between two people.

By all means, bring at least one copy of your résumé to the interview. Occasionally, at the close of an interview, an interviewer will express an interest in circulating a résumé to several departments, and you could then offer the copy you brought. Sometimes, an interview appointment provides an opportunity to meet others in the organization who may express an interest in you and your background, and it may be helpful to follow up with a copy of your résumé. Our best advice, however, is to keep it out of sight until needed or requested.

Employer Information

Whether your interview is for graduate school admission, an overseas corporate position, or a position with a local company, it is important to know something about the employer or the organization. Keeping in mind that the interview is relatively brief and that you will hopefully have other interviews with other organizations, it is important to keep your research in proportion. If secondary interviews are called for, you will have additional time to do further research. For the first interview, it is helpful to know the organization's mission, goals, size, scope of operations, and so forth. Your research may uncover recent areas of challenge or particular successes that may help to fuel the interview. Use the "What Do They Call the Job You Want?" section of Chapter 3, your library, and your career or guidance office to help you locate this information in the most efficient way possible. Don't be shy in asking advice of these counseling and guidance professionals on how best to spend your preparation time. With some practice, you'll soon learn how much information is enough and which kinds of information are most useful to you.

Interview Content

We've already discussed how it can help to think of the interview as an important conversation—one that, as with any conversation, you want to find pleasant and interesting and to leave you with a good feeling. But because this conversation is especially important, the information that's exchanged is critical to its success. What do you want them to know about you? What do you need to know about them? What interview technique do you need to particularly pay attention to? How do you want to manage the close of the interview? What steps will follow in the hiring process?

Except for the professional interviewer, most of us find interviewing stressful and anxiety-provoking. Developing a strategy before you begin interviewing will help you relieve some stress and anxiety. One particular strategy that has worked for many and may work for you is interviewing by objective. Before you interview, write down three to five goals you would like to achieve for that interview. They may be technique goals: smile a little more, have a firmer handshake, be sure to ask about the next stage in the interview process before leaving. They may be content-oriented goals: find out about the company's current challenges and opportunities; be sure to speak of your recent research, writing experiences, or foreign travel. Whatever your goals, jot down a few of them as goals for each interview.

Most people find that in trying to achieve these few goals, their interviewing technique becomes more organized and focused. After the interview, the most common question friends and family ask is "How did it go?" With this technique, you have an indication of whether you met *your* goals for the meeting, not just some vague idea of how it went. Chances are, if you accomplished what you wanted to, it improved the quality of the entire interview. As you continue to interview, you will want to revise your goals to continue improving your interview skills.

Now, add to the concept of the significant conversation the idea of a beginning, a middle, and a closing and you will have two thoughts that will give your interview a distinctive character. Be sure to make your introduction warm and cordial. Say your full name (and if it's a difficult-to-pronounce name, help the interviewer to pronounce it) and make certain you know your interviewer's name and how to pronounce it. Most interviews begin with some "soft talk" about the weather, chat about the candidate's trip to the interview site, or national events. This is done as a courtesy to relax both you and the interviewer, to get you talking, and to generally try to defuse the atmosphere of excessive tension. Try to be yourself, engage in the conversation, and don't try to second-guess the interviewer. This is simply what it appears to be— casual conversation.

Once you and the interviewer move on to exchange more serious information in the middle part of the interview, the two most important concerns become your ability to handle challenging questions and your success at asking meaningful ones. Interviewer questions will probably fall into one of three categories: personal assessment and career direction, academic assessment, and knowledge of the employer. Here are a few examples of questions in each category:

Personal Assessment and Career Direction
1. What motivates you to put forth your best effort?
2. What do you consider to be your greatest strengths and weaknesses?
3. What qualifications do you have that make you think you will be successful in this career?

Academic Assessment
1. What led you to choose your major?
2. What subjects did you like best and least? Why?
3. How has your college experience prepared you for this career?

Knowledge of the Employer
1. What do you think it takes to be successful in an organization like ours?
2. In what ways do you think you can make a contribution to our organization?
3. Why did you choose to seek a position with this organization?

The interviewer wants a response to each question but is also gauging your enthusiasm, preparedness, and willingness to communicate. In each response you should provide some information about yourself that can be related to the employer's needs. A common mistake is to give too much information. Answer each question completely, but be careful not to run on too long with extensive details or examples.

Questions About Underdeveloped Skills

Most employers interview people who have met some minimum criteria of education and experience. They interview candidates to see who they are, to learn what kind of personality they exhibit, and to get some sense of how they might fit into the existing organization. It may be that you are asked about skills the employer hopes to find and that you have not documented. Maybe it's statistical process control, experience with a specific simulation software tool, or knowledge of program controls strategies.

To questions about skills and experiences you don't have, answer honestly and forthrightly and try to offer some additional information about skills you do have. For example, perhaps the employer is disappointed you have no lean production experience. An honest answer may be as follows:

> *No, unfortunately, but I do understand lean principles. I attended a short course on the subject during my internship with Smith Manufacturing and did an independent study with Professor Jones on Toyota's production methodology. I think I could get up on the learning curve quickly.*

The employer hears an honest admission of lack of experience but is reassured by some specific skill details that do relate to lean production and a confident manner that suggests enthusiasm and interest in a challenge.

For many students, questions about their possible contribution to an employer's organization can prove challenging. Because your education has probably not included specific training for a job, you need to review your academic record and select capabilities you have developed in your major that an employer can appreciate. For example, perhaps you read well and can analyze and condense what you've read into smaller, more focused pieces. That could be valuable. Or maybe you did some serious research and you know you have valuable investigative skills. Your public speaking might be highly developed and you might use visual aids appropriately and effectively. Or maybe your skill at correspondence, memos, and messages is effective. Whatever it is, you must take it out of the academic context and put it into a new, employer-friendly context so your interviewer can best judge how you could help the organization.

Exhibiting knowledge of the organization will, without a doubt, show the interviewer that you are interested enough in the available position to have done some legwork in preparation for the interview. Remember, it is not necessary to know every detail of the organization's history but rather to have a general knowledge about why it is in business and how the industry is faring.

Sometime during the interview, generally after the midway point, you'll be asked if you have any questions for the interviewer. Your questions will tell the employer much about your attitude and your desire to understand the organization's expectations so you can compare them to your own strengths. The following are just a few questions you might want to ask:

1. What is the communication style of the organization? (meetings, memos, and so forth)
2. What would a typical day in this position be like for me?
3. What have been some of the interesting challenges and opportunities your organization has recently faced?

Most interviews draw to a natural closing point, so be careful not to prolong the discussion. At a signal from the interviewer, wind up your presentation, express your appreciation for the opportunity, and be sure to ask what the next stage in the process will be. When can you expect to hear from them? Will they be conducting second-tier interviews? If you are interested and haven't heard, would they mind a phone call? Be sure to collect a business card with the name and phone number of your interviewer. On your way out, you might have an opportunity to pick up organizational literature you haven't seen before.

With the right preparation—a thorough self-assessment, professional clothing, and employer information—you'll be able to set and achieve the goals you have established for the interview process.

Interview Follow-Up

Quite often there is a considerable time lag between interviewing for a position and being hired or, in the case of the networker, between your phone call or letter to a possible contact and the opportunity of a meeting. This can be frustrating. "Why aren't they contacting me?" "I thought I'd get another interview, but no one has telephoned." "Am I out of the running?" You don't know what is happening.

Consider the Differing Perspectives
Of course, there is another perspective—that of the networker or hiring organization. Organizations are complex, with multiple tasks that need to be accomplished each day. Hiring is a discrete activity that does not occur as

frequently as other job assignments. The hiring process might have to take second place to other, more immediate organizational needs. Although it may be very important to you, and it is certainly ultimately significant to the employer, other issues such as fiscal management, planning and product development, employer vacation periods, or financial constraints may prevent an organization or individual within that organization from acting on your employment or your request for information as quickly as you or they would prefer.

Use Your Communications Skills

Good communication is essential here to resolve any anxieties, and the responsibility is on you, the job or information seeker. Too many job seekers and networkers offer as an excuse that they don't want to "bother" the organization by writing letters or calling. Let us assure you here and now, once and for all, that if you are troubling an organization by over-communicating, someone will indicate that situation to you quite clearly. If not, you can only assume you are a worthwhile prospect and the employer appreciates being reminded of your availability and interest. Let's look at follow-up practices in the job interview process and the networking situation separately.

Following Up on the Employment Interview

A brief thank-you note following an interview is an excellent and polite way to begin a series of follow-up communications with a potential employer with whom you have interviewed and want to remain in touch. It should be just that—a thank-you for a good meeting. If you failed to mention some fact or experience during your interview that you think might add to your candidacy, you may use this note to do that. However, this should be essentially a note whose overall tone is appreciative and, if appropriate, indicative of a continuing interest in pursuing any opportunity that may exist with that organization. It is one of the few pieces of business correspondence that may be handwritten, but always use plain, good-quality, standard-size paper.

If, however, at this point you are no longer interested in the employer, the thank-you note is an appropriate time to indicate that. You are under no obligation to identify any reason for not continuing to pursue employment with that organization, but if you are so inclined to indicate your professional reasons (pursuing other employers more akin to your interests, looking for greater income production than this employer can provide, a different geographic location), you certainly may. It should not be written with an eye to negotiation, for it will not be interpreted as such.

As part of your interview closing, you should have taken the initiative to establish lines of communication for continuing information about your candidacy. If you asked permission to telephone, wait a week following your thank-you note, then telephone your contact simply to inquire how things are progressing on your employment status. The feedback you receive here should be taken at face value. If your interviewer simply has no information, he or she will tell you so and indicate whether you should call again and when. Don't be discouraged if this should continue over some period of time.

If during this time something occurs that you think improves or changes your candidacy (some new qualification or experience you may have had), including any offers from other organizations, by all means telephone or write to inform the employer about this. In the case of an offer from a competing but less desirable or equally desirable organization, telephone your contact, explain what has happened, express your real interest in the organization, and inquire whether some determination on your employment might be made before you must respond to this other offer. An organization that is truly interested in you may be moved to make a decision about your candidacy. Equally possible is the scenario in which they are not yet ready to make a decision and so advise you to take the offer that has been presented. Again, you have no ethical alternative but to deal with the information presented in a straightforward manner.

When accepting other employment, be sure to contact any employers still actively considering you and inform them of your new job. Thank them graciously for their consideration. There are many other job seekers out there just like you who will benefit from having their candidacy improved when others bow out of the race. Who knows, you might at some future time have occasion to interact professionally with one of the organizations with which you sought employment. How embarrassing it would be to have someone remember you as the candidate who failed to notify them that you were taking a job elsewhere!

In all of your follow-up communications, keep good notes of whom you spoke with, when you called, and any instructions that were given about return communications. This will prevent any misunderstandings and provide you with good records of what has transpired.

Job Offer Considerations

For many recent college graduates, the thrill of their first job and, for some, the most substantial regular income they have ever earned seems an excess of good fortune coming at once. To question that first income or to be critical in any way of the conditions of employment at the time of the initial offer seems like looking a gift horse in the mouth. It doesn't seem to occur to many new hires even to attempt to negotiate any aspect of their first job. And, as many employers who deal with entry-level jobs for recent college graduates will readily confirm, the reality is that there simply isn't much movement in salary available to these new college recruits. The entry-level hire generally does not have an employment track record on a professional level to provide any leverage for negotiation. Real negotiations on salary, benefits, retirement provisions, and so forth come to those with significant employment records at higher income levels.

Of course, the job offer is more than just money. It can be composed of geographic assignment, duties and responsibilities, training, benefits, health and medical insurance, educational assistance, car allowance or company vehicle, and a host of other items. All of this is generally detailed in the formal letter that presents the final job offer. In most cases this is a follow-up to a personal phone call from the employer representative who has been principally responsible for your hiring process.

That initial telephone offer is certainly binding as a verbal agreement, but most firms follow up with a detailed letter outlining the most significant parts of your employment contract. You may, of course, choose to respond immediately at the time of the telephone offer (which would be considered a binding oral contract), but you will also be required to formally answer the letter of offer with a letter of acceptance, restating the salient elements of the employer's description of your position, salary, and benefits. This ensures that both parties are clear on the terms and conditions of employment and remuneration and any other outstanding aspects of the job offer.

Is This the Job You Want?
Most new employees will respond affirmatively in writing, glad to be in the position to accept employment. If you've worked hard to get the offer and the job market is tight, other offers may not be in sight, so you will say, "Yes, I accept!" What is important here is that the job offer you accept be one that does fit your particular needs, values, and interests as you've outlined them in your self-assessment process. Moreover, it should be a job that will not only use your skills and education but also challenge you to develop new skills and talents.

Jobs are sometimes accepted too hastily, for the wrong reasons, and without proper scrutiny by the applicant. For example, an individual might readily accept a sales job only to find the continual rejection by potential clients unendurable. An office worker might realize within weeks the constraints of a desk job and yearn for more activity. Employment is an important part of our lives. It is, for most of our adult lives, our most continuous productive activity. We want to make good choices based on the right criteria.

If you have a low tolerance for risk, a job based on commission will certainly be very anxiety-provoking. If being near your family is important, issues of relocation could present a decision crisis for you. If you're an adventurous person, a job with frequent travel would provide needed excitement and be very desirable. The importance of income, the need to continue your education, your personal health situation—all of these have an impact on whether the job you are considering will ultimately meet your needs. Unless you've spent some time understanding and thinking about these issues, it will be difficult to evaluate offers you do receive.

More important, if you make a decision that you cannot tolerate and feel you must leave that job, you will then have both unemployment and self-esteem issues to contend with. These will combine to make the next job search tough going, indeed. So make your acceptance a carefully considered decision.

Negotiate Your Offer

It may be that there is some aspect of your job offer that is not particularly attractive to you. Perhaps there is no relocation allotment to help you move your possessions, and this presents some financial hardship for you. It may be that the health insurance is less than you had hoped. Your initial assignment may be different from what you expected, either in its location or in the duties and responsibilities that comprise it. Or it may simply be that the salary is less than you anticipated. Other considerations may be your official starting date of employment, vacation time, evening hours, dates of training programs or schools, and other concerns.

If you are considering not accepting the job because of some item or items in the job offer "package" that do not meet your needs, you should know that most employers emphatically wish that you would bring that issue to their attention. It may be that the employer can alter it to make the offer more agreeable for you. In some cases it cannot be changed. In any event the employer would generally like to have the opportunity to try to remedy a difficulty rather than risk losing a good potential employee over an issue that might have been resolved. After all, they have spent time and funds in securing your services, and they certainly deserve an opportunity to resolve any possible differences.

Honesty is the best approach in discussing any objections or uneasiness you might have over the employer's offer. Having received your formal offer in writing, contact your employer representative and indicate your particular dissatisfaction in a straightforward manner. For example, you might explain that while you are very interested in being employed by this organization, the salary (or any other benefit) is less than you have determined you require. State the terms you need, and listen to the response. You may be asked to put this in writing, or you may be asked to hold off until the firm can decide on a response. If you are dealing with a senior representative of the organization, one who has been involved in hiring for some time, you may get an immediate response or a solid indication of possible outcomes.

Perhaps the issue is one of relocation. Your initial assignment is in the Midwest, and because you had indicated a strong West Coast preference, you are surprised at the actual assignment. You might simply indicate that while you understand the need for the company to assign you based on its needs, you are disappointed and had hoped to be placed on the West Coast. You could inquire if that were still possible and, if not, would it be reasonable to expect a West Coast relocation in the future.

If your request is presented in a reasonable way, most employers will not see this as jeopardizing your offer. If they can agree to your proposal, they will. If not, they will simply tell you so, and you may choose to continue your candidacy with them or remove yourself from consideration. The choice will be up to you.

Some firms will adjust benefits within their parameters to meet the candidate's need if at all possible. If a candidate requires a relocation cost allowance, he or she may be asked to forgo tuition benefits for the first year to accomplish this adjustment. An increase in life insurance may be adjusted by some other benefit trade-off; perhaps a family dental plan is not needed. In these decisions you are called upon, sometimes under time pressure, to know how you value these issues and how important each is to you.

Many employers find they are more comfortable negotiating for candidates who have unique qualifications or who bring especially needed expertise to the organization. Employers hiring large numbers of entry-level college graduates may be far more reluctant to accommodate any changes in offer conditions. They are well supplied with candidates with similar education and experience so that if rejected by one candidate, they can draw new candidates from an ample labor pool.

Compare Offers

The condition of the economy, the job seeker's academic major and particular geographic job market, and individual needs and demands for certain employment conditions may not provide more than one job offer at a time. Some job seekers may feel that no reasonable offer should go unaccepted for the simple fear there won't be another.

In a tough job market, or if the job you seek is not widely available, or when your job search goes on too long and becomes difficult to sustain financially and emotionally, it may be necessary to accept an inferior offer. The alternative is continued unemployment. Even here, when you feel you don't have a choice, you can at least understand that in accepting this particular offer, there may be limitations and conditions you don't appreciate. At the time of acceptance, there were no other alternatives, but you can begin to use that position to gain the experience and talent to move toward a more attractive position.

Sometimes, however, more than one offer is received, and the candidate has the luxury of choice. If the job seeker knows what he or she wants and has done the necessary self-assessment honestly and thoroughly, it may be clear that one of the offers conforms more closely to those expressed wants and needs.

However, if, as so often happens, the offers are similar in terms of conditions and salary, the question then becomes which organization might provide the necessary climate, opportunities, and advantages for your professional development and growth. This is the time when solid employer research and astute questioning during the interviews really pay off. How much did you learn about the employer through your own research and skillful questioning? When the interviewer asked during the interview "Do you have any questions?" did you ask the kinds of questions that would help resolve a choice between one organization and another? Just as an employer must decide among numerous applicants, so must the applicant learn to assess the potential employer. Both are partners in the job search.

Reneging on an Offer

An especially disturbing occurrence for employers and career counseling professionals is when a job seeker formally (either orally or by written contract) accepts employment with one organization and later reneges on the agreement and goes with another employer.

There are all kinds of rationalizations offered for this unethical behavior. None of them satisfies. The sad irony is that what the job seeker is willing to do to the employer—make a promise and then break it—he or she would be outraged to have done to him- or herself: have the job offer pulled. It is a very bad way to begin a career. It suggests the individual has not taken the time to do the necessary self-assessment and self-awareness exercises to think and judge critically. The new offer taken may, in fact, be no better or worse than the one refused. You should be aware that there have been incidents of legal action following job candidates' reneging on an offer. This adds a very sour note to what should be a harmonious beginning of a lifelong adventure.

PART TWO

THE CAREER PATHS

5

Path I:
Teaching with an
Advanced Degree

Everyone who has gone to college has seen what professors do. Your own sociology professors have probably inspired as well as informed you during your undergraduate years. You've seen them in action: lecturing and grading papers, pursuing their own research, and fulfilling other academic roles. Perhaps one of your college teachers has suggested that you pursue an advanced degree and seek work as a professor yourself. It is a natural progression, as more than two-thirds of the sociologists working in this country teach in colleges and universities. And life in academia reaches beyond the classroom, as many sociologists are also involved in research, consulting, and other aspects of public life.

The overall field of college teaching is a large one. According to the U.S. Department of Education, postsecondary teachers held nearly 1.7 million jobs in 2006. Of course, sociology is just one small part of that enterprise, but it is an important one. After all, most colleges offer at least some sociology courses. At a small community college, the curriculum may be limited to one or two introductory sociology courses. At a large university, on the other hand, enough courses may be offered to support full-scale bachelor's, master's, or doctoral programs.

For example, Missouri State University has nearly forty different sociology courses in its curriculum, including those listed below, all of which must be staffed by qualified faculty. While not all courses are offered each academic term, some are offered in multiple sections to accommodate student demand.

Introduction to Society
Social Problems

Social Movements
Sociology of Gender Roles
Special Topics
Service Learning in Sociology
Research Methodology
Statistics for Social Research
Sociology of Education
Work, Industry, and Society
Social Deviance
Rural Sociology
The Family
Urban Sociology
Introduction of Social Theory
Feminist Theories of Social Order
Race and Ethnic Group Relations
Medical Sociology
Sociology of Childhood
Sociology of Sport
The Individual in Society
Sociology of Law
Religion in Society
Special Topics
Social Inequality
Advanced Social Theory
Society and the Future
Population Analysis
Directed Readings in Sociology
Sociological Research
Gender in Global Community
Community Change
Sociology of Religion

Teaching can be an appealing career choice. To pursue ideas and theories, accumulate and disseminate information, and influence the intellectual development of countless students over the years provides many rewards. In the classroom, learning occurs for instructors as well as students. Most teachers readily admit they enjoy being students themselves, and good teachers come to the classroom as ready to learn from students as students arrive hoping to learn from their teachers. Good teachers maintain a regular program of professional development, adding to their body of knowledge, continuing to learn new classroom techniques, and improving their teaching methods.

The life of an academic provides for a nice balance between time spent working independently and time spent with others. Hours are spent reviewing literature, writing lectures, and grading papers and exams. At the same time, however, the life of a teacher allows for a great deal of intellectual exchange. Collaboration on research projects, team teaching, and institutional committees combine and recombine faculty colleagues and students as they move toward common goals.

Any sociology professor will tell you a surprising fact about the profession and teachers. They don't teach sociology, they teach students! The art of teaching and the skills required to handle the dynamics of student interaction are as important as knowledge of the course content. Your classroom will be populated by many students majoring in sociology. Their responses to your presentations are important factors in their ongoing commitment to this major. You'll also have many nonsociology majors who are taking your course as a general education requirement or for a minor. Students of diverse ages, cultural backgrounds, and biases sit in your class with dramatically different degrees of interest in the subject and the teacher. With all those variables, simply having a love of sociology yourself is not enough; commitment to teaching is essential.

Most college teaching candidates will repeatedly encounter that phrase: "a strong commitment to teaching is essential." You will be expected to demonstrate that commitment to the classroom with recommendations by those who have observed your teaching, with student and peer evaluations of your classroom, and by teaching a sample instructional unit to faculty during an on-campus job interview.

Successful teaching requires more than knowledge in a subject area. The world is full of extremely knowledgeable people who, for one reason or another and quite often inexplicably, cannot transmit that knowledge to others.

Planning for learning outcomes is a good example of a critical teaching skill. Teaching sociology within an established college curriculum means your course content must correspond to departmental goals and course outlines. A written course description will be in the catalog (in print, online, or both). To cover this body of learning within a set time period requires judicious planning of the material. What will be done each day? How much time is to be allowed between assignments, readings, and labs? What materials should be required and what others should only be recommended? Scores of decisions must be made about how material will be introduced and presented and about how you will evaluate your students.

Consider, also, that students learn in different ways. Some are auditory learners who enjoy listening and gain most of their information in this way. They may not learn as much from printed materials as from oral lectures and discussions in class. They may even need to audiotape your lecture in lieu of taking notes if this process is too awkward for them. Others prefer a visual approach with board work, videos, web-based information, handouts, their own notes, diagrams, books, and many visual materials. They retain these images and can call them up to remember the material. Still others need to participate through role plays, team projects, and other activities that physically involve them. These are kinesthetic learners, and they are often forgotten in planning and curriculum design. The professional teacher ensures that his or her class is satisfying the learning styles of all the students through judicious combinations of modalities in teaching. Professional teachers analyze their own teaching and seek to incorporate teaching styles that come less naturally to them to ensure they reach all their students.

What happens in a classroom is not static. The classroom is an emotionally charged environment for the student and instructor. For students, issues of self-esteem and competency frequently surface. Students are exploring their self-image—their capabilities, values, and achievements. A good professor understands this and encourages a risk-free environment of mutual appreciation and participation. Both teacher and student are allowed to make mistakes and move on. The professor strives to assist in establishing congruence between the student's self (who I know I am right now), the ideal self (who I want to be), and the learning environment being created in the classroom.

Issues of competency, self-esteem, and self-worth are closely associated with the basics of evaluation and grading. Grades are an expected and required part of many institutional academic settings. Establishing fair and consistent standards for evaluating your students and assigning grades is a significant challenge to many professors who otherwise feel perfectly competent in the teaching role. Fair and intellectually respectable test design and construction is an art and science deserving of a professor's attention. Students often complain about the grading practices of teachers they, in every other respect, feel positively about.

Professors are called upon to fill other roles, too. Animating the class and inspiring attention and commitment to the material are all required in teaching. One factor in this is the professor's enthusiasm. Another factor is teaching style, including the effective use of ancillary materials and the ability to relate this material and other course elements to a student's life.

Each class is an opportunity to not only teach the subject sociology, but also to teach students how to learn. Routinely, professors should be helping students learn how to question, how to record information, how to be selective in focusing their research, and how to retain information.

Most of all, an instructor will evaluate and, by example, develop the student's capacity for self-evaluation through careful, caring feedback about both in- and out-of-class work. The instructor's own example of preparation, organization, personal appearance, evaluation standards, student interest, and enthusiasm will remain an example long after the memory of the actual class content may have faded.

Teachers are very frequently cited as important factors when people choose careers. Very often, teachers will remember one or two of their teachers who were strong influences on their decision to teach. Much of that influence was a result of the teacher's presence in the classroom: serving as a model of someone enjoying what he or she was doing and doing it skillfully. The teacher was professional and correct yet remained natural and approachable. Students could watch and listen and think, "Yes, that is what I want to do."

Definition of the Career Path

A bachelor's degree in sociology is just the starting point if your goal is teaching at a college or university. Unless you are working as a teaching assistant, all such positions require a master's or doctoral degree. There are more opportunities for those students who have continued on to the doctoral level, particularly at the more prestigious public and private universities. However, depending on your area of specialization, you can also find many instances in which a master's degree is sufficient. This is because academic institutions are interested in finding candidates who have expertise in a certain area of sociology. Thus, many faculty position descriptions are specific about the research interests the institution hopes an applicant will bring to their campus.

You may enter a doctoral program that does not necessarily require a stopping-off point at the master's level. Doing this represents a major commitment of your time, your finances, and your belief in the resources of your graduate school.

Or you may decide to begin your graduate work with a master's degree and then reevaluate your position before launching yourself on the doctoral course. This allows you to receive a credential for your first two years of graduate work and provides a resting place from which you can survey the future.

Do you want to stop with your master's degree for a year or two to work, continue on immediately in the same institution for your doctoral degree, or change schools?

For many, university affiliation changes between the master's and doctoral degrees. This change may be due to a desire for a particular field of study, the wish to work with a new group of sociology professionals, or the resources (scholarly, financial, or geographic) of a new graduate school.

Areas of Specialization

Sociologists study human society and social behavior by examining the groups and social institutions that people form. These include families, tribes, communities, and governments, as well as a variety of social, religious, political, and business organizations. Sociologists study the behavior and interaction of groups, trace their origin and growth, and analyze the influence of group activities on individual members. Some sociologists are concerned primarily with the characteristics of social groups and institutions. Others are more interested in the ways individuals are affected by the groups to which they belong.

Teachers of sociology can focus their research and teaching efforts in at least one of many different areas. The following list is by no means inclusive.

Community sociology
Complex organizations
Computer applications in social science
Courtship and marriage
Criminology
Cross-cultural studies
Delinquency
Deviance
Dynamics of human populations
Environmental sociology
Ethnic studies
Gender/sexuality
General sociology
Gerontology
Health/illness sociology
History of sociology
Immigration intervention strategies
Minority groups
Online social networking

Poverty
Small group processes
Social change
Social control
Social policy
Social problems
Social stratification
Social theory
Sociolinguistics
Sociology of cyberspace
Sociology of law
Sociology of race
Statistics methods
Substance abuse
Urban sociology
Urban rural sociology
Youth services

While you may be familiar with some of these areas of specialization from your undergraduate survey courses, others may be completely foreign. It can be a bewilderingly long list. Even if some of these specialties do seem interesting, you are probably asking yourself, "How do I become knowledgeable about these areas?" The answer, in most cases, is in the early days of your graduate degree work. Your graduate work will expose you to a number of other graduate students, each of whom has his or her own perspective on the study of sociology and personal research interests. The intellectual sharing that goes on during graduate programs will stimulate your own reading and research into many of these specialty areas. Your graduate faculty members will also have specific areas of interest in which they actively research and publish the results of that research and fieldwork.

Master's-Level Teaching Positions

While most teaching positions at colleges and universities require a doctorate, there are many college positions for those holding a master's degree in sociology. The *Chronicle for Higher Education*, the weekly newspaper reporting on higher education issues, provides the most complete listing of faculty, staff, and leadership position openings for colleges and universities in the United States, Canada, and some foreign countries. Here you will find listings for positions that accept the master's degree in sociology, including jobs at state universities, community colleges, technical colleges, and private colleges, as well as for nonacademic positions. The following job description presents specific demands for area expertise within sociology as well.

Tenure-Track Position, Sociology. Nine-month appointment. Minimum of master's in sociology required. Experience teaching in a community college preferred. Ability to teach Introduction to Sociology and other courses such as Social Problems, Urban Sociology, Race and Ethnicity, Gerontology, etc. Ability to teach in a second discipline preferred.

You can find similar positions, even those requiring a high level of specialization, in satellite campuses of state colleges that offer two-year degrees or in colleges with smaller enrollments. With a master's degree, it is possible to have a rewarding career teaching sociology at the college level. Two-year programs and community college work can provide a long and productive career within the same institution or provide the opportunity for a lateral move to a similar type of institution. Note, however, that if you are interested in moving from that type of institution to a four-year college or university, it may be difficult without an advanced degree, despite your years of teaching experience.

There are also some jobs teaching at the four-year college level with a master's degree in sociology. Nevertheless, the trend in these schools, the expectation, and the market demand is for the doctoral degree. A doctorate will provide you with the most employment security and the most opportunities for a teaching career at the college and university level.

The Doctoral Degree

Students who pursue a doctorate in sociology will find a wider range of opportunities in the world of academia. Yet even at this level, competition is keen.

The road to a Ph.D. is fairly long and arduous. It is hard work, requiring sustained effort and commitment. And despite fellowships and teaching assistantships, it can also be expensive. Many doctoral students juggle heavy academic demands with jobs that leave them fatigued and not always able to meet their financial needs. At the same time, friends may be well along in their careers and beginning to raise families or enjoy the other benefits of being established in a career. This can be frustrating to doctoral students who are now several years older than when they began, perhaps tired of being the student, and wanting to get started on a real job. Both men and women in doctoral programs have to make decisions about relationships, marriage, children, and other significant events that will affect their pursuit of the Ph.D.

Along the way, you'll meet some wonderful people: fellow graduate students and faculty from your own department and other academic areas. Some of these friends and colleagues will remain friends the rest of your life. Even colleagues separated by long distances with only an e-mail connection have the opportunity to catch up at conferences and symposia. In a long teaching career, it is not uncommon to change employers, and you may find yourself crossing paths with old friends.

Building and maintaining this network of relationships can play an important role in your job search after you have earned your Ph.D. and even later in your career. Your friends and colleagues will apprise you of position openings early and marshal the necessary support, recommendations, and documentation you may need to successfully compete for jobs and tenure.

Value of the Earned Doctorate

Although a doctorate is frequently the ultimate goal of those who aspire to an academic career, many graduate students begin their search for placement before having completed their Ph.D. While some openings require that you already have your dissertation completed and your doctoral degree in hand, some advertisements will encourage the application of what are informally known as All But Dissertation (ABD) candidates—those who have not yet but soon will complete their degree work.

A position requiring an earned doctorate will pay more than an ABD position and will lead more quickly and directly to possible tenure and promotion. The ABD candidates will also have to decide how they will finish their degrees (the dissertation often being the most time-consuming aspect of their academics) while holding down a full-time job.

Especially in sociology, because of the sensitive nature of the material being presented, college and universities of even modest size seek the most credentialed and skilled faculty they can find and afford. Larger and more prestigious schools with significant research agendas are even more demanding of the backgrounds of their faculty.

You'll have opportunities to write, teach, and perhaps publish all before you finish your degree. Take advantage of these opportunities when you can. As job advertisements suggest, these qualifications may be desired. Be careful, however, because it is possible to become overly involved in some of these areas to the detriment of your degree progress.

Beyond the Degree: Other Qualities of Teachers of Sociology

Issues of importance to both master's and doctoral degree holders include the following:

- Teaching effectiveness
- Research, publications, and presentations
- Cultural sensitivity
- Community service

Position descriptions, such as those found in scholarly publications, allow the sociology graduate considering a teaching career to approach the hiring process with eyes wide open! A close reading of these advertisements indicates not only the degree of specialization that is demanded, but also the institutional values for teaching, publication, community outreach, and collaboration that must be demonstrated and met. Getting a college teaching position requires much, much more than a doctoral degree.

Teaching Effectiveness

Quite often, job announcements include a request for documentation of teaching success. Graduate teaching assistantships obtained while working on your doctoral degree provide this experience. Or you can acquire this experience from part-time faculty, lecturer, or adjunct faculty positions taken at other colleges or programs while engaged in your doctoral studies. Summaries of student teaching evaluations that you received can be used to document your teaching success.

Research, Publications, and Presentations

Community colleges and some four-year colleges emphasize the teaching role and do not put excessive demands on faculty to "publish or perish." But other institutions do value research and publications very highly, and faculty put forth a determined effort to find good research projects and then publish them. This is, in fact, the norm at comprehensive universities, liberal arts colleges with a research tradition, and some other institutions.

Regardless of the posture of your institution vis-á-vis research and publications, as a teacher you should have an interest in sharing what you know with a larger audience, perhaps through writing books, articles, or monographs. Or you may prefer public presentations at seminars, workshops, and conferences.

When being considered for promotion and tenure, your record of sharing your technical and professional expertise will be examined.

Diversity Awareness
Profound cultural sensitivity and awareness is insistent and pervasive throughout teaching communities, but especially focused in sociology classrooms where the subject is apt to be individual and group behaviors.

If you were teaching in a multicultural class with an Asian complement, for example, it would be highly inappropriate—and a good example of cultural bias—to indicate in a class discussion on symptomatic behavior that a failure to make direct and sustained eye contact with a physician was significant. Many Asian cultures do not make direct eye contact with strangers and, even more seldom, with authority figures.

Gender-biased language, ignorance of cultures and customs, or an inconsiderate choice of texts or illustrative materials from a diversity perspective only serves to impugn your teaching and undermine your credibility. It is in your best interest to broaden your horizons and ensure that your classroom is an inclusive and welcoming one.

Community Service
In addition to their other roles, colleges and universities have always been part of the larger communities in which they reside. Faculty and staff are often called upon to contribute to the school's community. These contributions can take many forms, including anything from participating in annual cleanup days to allowing local organizations to use space for special events.

Because of the nature of sociology, the need and opportunities for sociology faculty to engage in outreach is great. Local counseling hotlines may need staffers or someone to train them. Homeless shelters or halfway houses often need skilled volunteers to take client histories or do referrals with other helping agencies. Teen drop-in sex-information clinics, local civic groups needing speakers, a variety of board of trustee opportunities—all of these could benefit from the sociology faculty member's involvement and attention.

The Long Road to a Ph.D.
Earning a doctorate definitely presents a major challenge. Even the best students often find the process daunting. While completion times vary, it takes several years of study beyond the bachelor's level to earn a Ph.D. or other doctoral degree. This includes not just fulfilling the necessary course requirements, but also completion of a dissertation.

There has been considerable discussion in academic circles about the number of individuals who begin doctoral programs and do not see them through to completion. In fact, Neil Rudenstine, a former president of Harvard University, coauthored a book on the issue of improving and tightening up the time requirements to earn a Ph.D., particularly in the humanities and social sciences. His research clearly demonstrated that the timeline between initiating the Ph.D. degree and earning it (elapsed time-to-degree), in candidates earning a social science degree (which includes sociology), was seven and a half years. In addition, not all students who begin a Ph.D. program complete it, so a correspondingly high rate of mortality goes along with this issue of time-to-degree.

Doctoral work comes at a time in many young people's lives when, after sixteen or more years of education, no matter how fascinating the advanced study, distractions occur. These might be relationships, a desire to begin a family, economic pressures to leave school and earn an income, or simply fatigue. Consequently, the dropout rate for students has been high, especially when doctoral programs are not sufficiently explicit about requirements and the time it takes to complete a degree.

The Working Environment

Just what is it like to teach sociology at the college level? The working conditions for sociology professors may vary somewhat according to the institution, but there is enough commonality of experience to allow some generalizations. Many people consider a college teaching environment one of the most attractive work settings imaginable. There is less need to appease a number of outside publics. There are no school boards to satisfy, no parents, no parent-teacher groups. Students are there voluntarily, and the upper-level classes are populated with sociology majors who love their subject and are interested in doing the work required to succeed in their courses.

Typical Schedule

Teaching time in a four-year college or university setting typically involves about six to twelve class hours taught per week, while community college faculty may teach fifteen hours a week or more. At an institution that focuses on faculty research, the professor is responsible for teaching two to three courses that each meet two to three hours per week. Schools that emphasize teaching rather than research require instructors to teach three to four courses for a total of nine to twelve hours of class meetings per week. These class hours and some mandated office hours for advising students are the principal requirements for attendance on the faculty member's part. They hardly tell the whole story of the work schedule because they do not include the many, many hours that most faculty members put into doing scholarly research, an important component of an academic career. Depending on their schedule in a given academic term, they might be found working as many as thirty hours a week investigating and writing research articles and books.

Unlike some work environments, teaching college does not involve following a rigid daily routine. Class schedules are the fixed element; beyond those, much is up to the involvement and activity level of the individual faculty member. Certainly, it can be busy and long. Professors may feel institutional and professional pressures to fulfill certain roles, but the actual election of how to do that is up to the individual. There will be classes, office hours, meetings, and research work to do. Because college campuses are often wonderful centers of art, music, and intellectual exchange, there are frequently events to attend in the evening. Faculty members may also act as advisors to fraternities, sororities, campus newspapers, or clubs, all of which will certainly add hours to the workday.

A less well-known aspect of academic life is the number of faculty members who work part-time for the college or university. These instructors, sometimes referred to as "adjunct faculty," may have other, primary jobs in areas such as government, private industry or services, and nonprofit research.

Administrative Roles

Some faculty members move on to administrative roles or take them on temporarily and then return to full-time teaching or research.

In some departments, the role of chair of the department is rotated, and all faculty are expected to serve a term. In other institutions, the chair is a hotly contested office.

Department chair duties involve overseeing the scheduling of each semester's courses and assigning faculty responsibility for those course offerings. Duties may also include hiring part-time faculty and adjuncts to meet demand or replace faculty on sabbatical as well as negotiations with other administrators for additional classroom space.

Supervision of the department budget is the chair's responsibility, and this includes monitoring expenditures for supplies, special events, faculty development, and travel. There is often intense faculty lobbying for travel and professional development funds from the chair, who must exercise impartiality and discretion in administering these funds.

Department meetings are called and run by the chair, who also sets the meeting agenda. Meeting frequency is often a function of the size of a department and generally ranges from weekly to monthly.

Many colleges and universities hold a council of chairs to address issues such as curriculum change, general education requirements, faculty standards, and other interrelated issues.

Serving on Committees

Serving on committees is an expected role of every faculty member. This work is important because the faculty at most colleges are the governing and rule-making bodies who determine and vote on governance and program changes. Committee work can be issue oriented, such as a commission on the status of women or a female faculty pay-equity survey. It may be programmatic, such as a committee to study the core curriculum for undergraduates or to devise a new graphic arts major. Or it may be related to credentials, as in a committee set up to prepare materials for an accreditation visit.

Some committees—such as academic standards, curriculum review, promotion and tenure, planning, and administrator review—are permanent, though the members may change on a rotating schedule. Other committees are formed for a limited time or until the completion of some task. These ad hoc committees are essential and are one vehicle for guiding the direction of the school. For the faculty, having the support of all the faculty and a constant supply of fresh and interested members helps to ensure all voices are heard and many different opinions considered in making what are often long-reaching decisions.

Instructional Support

Support services and facilities, including laboratories, tend to be excellent for college faculty. Support staff are often available to process materials, do copying, and prepare testing materials. A private office is usually provided, and there may be quite a varied menu of faculty privileges. Computers are provided for writing, research, website design, library access, and data manipulation.

Teaching Introductory Courses

Most advertisements indicate that the successful candidate will be teaching general sociology classes. Teaching Introduction to Sociology classes is usually part of the teaching load of new college sociology faculty. Many students take Introduction to Sociology because it is a college requirement for graduation and part of a general-education core curriculum, not because they are sociology majors or have deliberately chosen the course. In offering this course, the sociology department performs a service to the entire college. Of course, this introductory course may prove to be an exciting introduction to a field of study many students had not previously considered. Undecided students often base their choice of major on the introduction provided by these required courses. Even senior faculty will teach at least one offering of Introduction to Sociology, though as you become more senior in the faculty you can take on courses more directly related to your interests and educational background.

The Research Role

In addition to courses and advising, scholarly research is an expectation even at those colleges for whom tenure is not based on publication. All colleges want their faculty to contribute to the scholarly dialogue in their disciplines; this is reviewed by chairs of departments and academic deans periodically throughout your career. It may be a determining element in granting tenure or promotion and may influence issues such as salary negotiations and merit increases.

Tenure

An added protection is the granting of tenure—a lifetime appointment at a given university—to established professors who have documented significant teaching histories and excellent student reviews, publications, campus committee work, and outreach to the community. Tenure gives professors an additional degree of job security and further supports their expression of academic freedom. It must be kept in mind that colleges and universities have strict guidelines for promotion and tenure. At many schools, faculty members are under significant pressure to write, do research, deliver papers at professional meetings, and become involved in outreach to the community and in college service to rise in academic rank or even hold their positions.

With higher education struggling to cut costs, however, this practice has come under scrutiny. In times of economic challenge, administrators often must cut budgets, and one easy way is by replacing retiring tenured faculty or departmental tenured faculty with nontenured personnel. The fewer tenure budget lines on the accounting sheet, the more flexible the budget.

The Right Qualifications

Most four-year colleges and universities require that job candidates possess a doctorate in sociology and, in addition, usually look for specialized areas of research, publication, or prior teaching and/or clinical experience. Occasionally, a college will hire a faculty member on a nontenured basis with less than a doctoral degree, but generally, the larger the institution, the less likely this will be the case. Salary and assignments may be affected by lack of an earned doctorate.

If you are hired without an earned doctoral degree, the contract at hiring may stipulate how much time can elapse before the degree must be earned. The difficulty here is finishing the degree (for many the dissertation is the most challenging and time-consuming aspect of the degree) while holding down a full-time job. This certainly needs to be considered in your negotiations. You might set a tentative date for Ph.D. completion, to be reviewed and finalized after your first year of teaching.

In community colleges, a master's degree may be sufficient. Many community college faculty do hold doctoral degrees, so in a competitive situation, a candidate with a terminal degree may win out. But it is not normally an absolute requirement.

Seasoned scholars work with students at the very senior levels of graduate work for both master's and doctoral degrees. These scholars enhance their own unique areas of expertise as students pursue their degrees. Classes may be very small at this level, even at a large university, and the work is highly collaborative. At this level, your teaching work may be reduced to allow for pure research and writing in your areas of interest and scholarship, and you are likely to be called upon frequently to speak to professional and scholarly groups about that research.

Earnings

College professors earn excellent salaries. According to the U.S. Department of Labor, median annual earnings of all postsecondary teachers in 2006 were $56,120.

Actual salaries vary widely. Major factors influencing pay for college professors include rank, type of institution, geographic area, and the academic field being taught. According to a 2006–2007 survey by the American Association of University Professors, salaries for full-time faculty averaged $73,207, with average salaries by rank as follows:

Professors: $98,974
Associate professors: $69,911
Assistant professors: $58,662
Instructors: $42,609
Lecturers: $48,289

Salaries in Canada tend to be similar to those in the United States, averaging C$65,665 in 2007, according to Service Canada. (Of course, differences in U.S. and Canadian currency should be taken into account, along with differences due to geographical location and type of institution.)

On average, faculty members in four-year colleges and universities earn higher salaries than do those who teach in two-year institutions. Those in technical disciplines or fields where those outside of the academic arena earn high salaries, such as engineering, medicine, and law, may earn more than those in the liberal arts or education.

Along with their basic salaries, many faculty members add to their salaries by taking on consulting jobs, teaching additional courses, writing for publication, or other professional activities. They also tend to earn very good benefits. At some private institutions, this even includes free or reduced tuition for family members.

Career Outlook

The traditional college-age population of eighteen- to twenty-four-year-olds has continued increasing, leading to a corresponding need for an increase in the number of college-level teachers. In addition, a significant number of adults are returning to college. As a result, demand for college teachers is expected to increase, although the growing use of part-time faculty may limit growth in new jobs.

An interesting development is the growth of distance learning, particularly over the Internet. This method of learning appeals to those who live in remote areas or whose family and work responsibilities prohibit them from enrolling in full-time programs. The United States has expanded its offering of distance learning opportunities to enlisted men and women. These new technological developments, however, will only be as useful as the information that can be imparted via these new methods, leading to a demand for online teachers at both traditional colleges and universities as well as at new online institutions.

Strategy for Finding the Jobs

Obviously, the first step in pursuing a college teaching career is to acquire the necessary educational credentials. But once you've taken it this far, you will certainly want to employ an equally intelligent and thorough strategy toward finding the right job. This strategy should include being prepared to relocate, getting your curriculum vitae in shape, using well-established job listings such as the *Chronicle of Higher Education*, networking with faculty colleagues, and attending professional meetings. Be sure to enhance your strategy as you decide on the area of sociology you will specialize in by talking with mentors and career development professionals.

Willingness to Relocate

If you want to land a college teaching position in sociology, you will probably have to relocate to an institution other than where you received your degree. Higher education has limited openings at any one time. You will increase your opportunities for securing a teaching post as you expand the boundaries of where you will consider relocating.

Like many graduate students, you may have enjoyed some part-time teaching employment at your degree-granting institution. Occasionally, an opportunity to teach as an adjunct faculty member for a limited period might be available. Adjunct positions are often used to staff introductory courses or to fill in a shortage during national searches for permanent full-time faculty. Adjunct or part-time work is a wonderful experience and will be an excellent recommendation or means to a recommendation to an institution considering your application. It is seldom, however, a guarantee of earning a full-time spot at your own school.

Consequently, though there may be schools where you would enjoy teaching or areas of the country where you would prefer to live, the supply and demand of college professorships clearly dictate that you must follow the demand and relocate.

It may be disappointing to feel your job search is completely dictated by marketplace demands. However, most faculty members have relocated, and many mention their real pleasure at discovering a new area of the country, bringing them new activities, experiences, and professional and personal relationships, as they have moved with their careers. College communities the world over tend to be centers of exchange, with speakers, arts events, celebrations, and a year-round calendar of activities for people of all ages and interests. Because of the college population, many have good shopping and excellent services. Most college communities are wonderful places in which to live, raise a family, and retire.

Locating Job Openings

Job openings in academia are always advertised. A favorite publication of both colleges and job seekers is the *Chronicle of Higher Education*. This is a weekly, national publication that lists community college, four-year college, and university teaching positions in a wide range of fields, including sociology. Many of these advertisements are large display ads that detail in full the requirements and duties of the positions advertised. This publication is readily available on college campuses. Your career center, department office, and college library will all have copies you can review each week.

The *Chronicle*'s job advertisements are also available online, and entire electronic editions are often accessible on public campus computer networks, thus making it easy to print out copies of announcements that interest you. Check out these offerings at chronicle.com. Other resources of this type include Academic Careers Online (academiccareers.com) and HigherEdJobs.com (higheredjobs.com).

Importance of Networking

Aside from your credentials themselves, perhaps the most important foundation for finding a college-level position will be the faculty contacts you make as you pursue your advanced degree. This well-established network becomes very active when schools are filling positions. Many search committees rely on the personal recommendations of friends or former teaching associates as the best sources of information on candidates.

Keep in mind that this is a referral network, not a placement service. Your colleagues will be suggesting your name as an applicant. There are no guarantees, and all positions at this level must go through a search committee and interviews. Nevertheless, a request from a faculty colleague to apply for a teaching vacancy is a strong beginning.

For this reason, it's important to ensure that your faculty mentors and colleagues are well aware of your teaching and research interests and your geographic preferences so they can speak on your behalf when they hear of an opening that might suit your research background and teaching experience.

Professional Meetings

If possible, be sure to attend academic conferences, professional meetings, and seminars (on your own campus as well as at other institutions). Attending such events will allow you to meet and listen to representatives from many institutions. You will become aware of research initiatives and many of the current issues in academe. Familiar faces will begin to appear as you continue on the conference circuit. Don't hesitate to submit your own proposals for presentations. These are good opportunities to share your scholarship and demonstrate your willingness to do outreach.

Job interviews may also be conducted at professional meetings. Position openings for which interviews are being held are posted in a conspicuous place at the conference registration table. As a graduate student, many of these conferences are available to you at substantially reduced fees, and you should take advantage of them for the professional content and the opportunity to meet representatives from the departments of other higher education institutions.

Potential Employers

Even though it is helpful to have a network of colleagues who are keeping their ears tuned for news of job openings, the positions themselves are always advertised. There is no hidden job market in academia, and the listings are usually widely distributed. The following resources can provide the names of potential employers.

• **Directories.** There are several directories that will help you identify institutions where you could teach sociology. These compendiums contain far too many listings for even the most ambitious mass mailing, but they will help you locate schools by size, number of faculty, geographic location, and so forth. They include *Peterson's Two-Year Colleges*, *Peterson's Four-Year Colleges*, *Peterson's Graduate Schools in the U.S.*, and *The College Board Book of Majors and Graduate Degrees*.

• **Career office postings.** Career offices often carry national job vacancy listings that include teaching positions. Some of these listings include *Current Jobs for Graduates in Education* and *Current Jobs for Graduates* (both at graduatejobs.com), as well as the *Chronicle of Higher Education* (chronicle .com). Many career offices also receive individual job posting fliers directly from institutions looking to hire sociology faculty. Be sure to find out if your institution receives these notices.

• **College websites.** Most colleges and universities post job openings on their websites. Check the institution's home page for headings such as "Jobs" or "Human Resources," and then look under "Faculty Openings" or a similar subhead.

• **Sociology department postings.** Sometimes when a hiring institution is seeking to fill a position under time pressure, it will send notices of openings to every school offering a graduate program in sociology. Be sure to find out where the sociology department posts these notices at your school. Often you'll find them on a bulletin board near the department chair's office or the department secretary's desk.

• **Professional associations.** In addition, be sure to carefully review the list of professional associations for teachers of sociology later in this chapter. For several associations, the line labeled "Job Listings" covers any activities that the association undertakes to assist its members in finding employment. These include professional meetings for sharing résumés, newsletters that contain job openings or positions wanted, and advertising space in journals.

Possible Job Titles

Job titles for positions relating to teaching and research in sociology will be fairly standard; typical examples include professor, instructor, faculty member, researcher. Position descriptions will list areas of educational and research specialization required for the position. In both teaching and research, a specialization can be developed in one of the following fields.

Clinical sociology
Comparative sociology
Educational sociology
Historical sociology
Industrial sociology
Microsociology
Organizational sociology
Phenomenological sociology
Political sociology
Sociolinguistics
Sociological jurisprudence
Visual sociology

Professional Associations

Professional associations are sometimes the best-kept secret of the job search. Raising the level of professional employment in their area of expertise is one of the goals of most of these organizations. No matter which occupation you choose to enter, at least one association will exist to serve your professional needs. Some of these associations will be able to assist you by providing possible leads for networking or actual job listings. Look for those groups that have membership directories or some type of job listing service. For the most part you will have to join an association to take full advantage of related services, but if you know which field you want to enter, consider it an investment in your future.

Probably the best single information resource for someone considering a career in teaching sociology at the college or university level is the American Sociological Association. Students are eligible to join at reduced rates, and by doing so they can begin the ever-important tasks of networking and gaining an insight on working as a professional in this field. Review the other associations to see if you feel they can assist you in your job search.

Alpha Kappa Delta
Box U-1147
Mobile, AL 36688
alpha-kappa-delta.org
Members/Purpose: Honorary society in sociology. Sponsors undergraduate paper competitions, holds research symposia.
Publications: Handbook, newsletter, *Sociological Inquiry*
Training: Holds symposia
Job Listings: None

American Sociological Association (ASA)
1307 New York Avenue NW,
   Suite 700
Washington, DC 20005
asanet.org
Members/Purpose: Sociologists, social scientists, and others interested in research, teaching, and application of sociology; graduate and undergraduate sociology students who are sponsored by a member of the association.
Publications: Offers wide range of publications including *American Sociological Review, Social Psychology, Footnotes, Journal of Health and Social Behavior, Rose Series in Sociology*
Training: Holds conferences and other meetings
Job Listings: Offers online Job Bank

Association of Black Sociologists (ABS)
4200 Wisconsin Avenue NW
PMB 106-257
Washington, DC 20016
blacksociologists.org

Members/Purpose: Promotes the professional interests of black sociologists; promotes an increase in the number of professionally trained sociologists; helps stimulate and improve the quality of research and the teaching of sociology; provides perspectives regarding black experiences as well as expertise for understanding and dealing with problems confronting black people; protects professional rights and safeguards civil rights stemming from executing the above objectives.
Publications: *The Griot* (newsletter), roster of membership
Training: Sponsors conferences
Job Listings: Offers online Career Center

Association for Humanist Sociology (AHS)

altrue.net/site/humanist
(Mailing address changes yearly; see website for contact information)
Members/Purpose: Sociologists, social scientists, social workers, and others interested in humanistic sociology. Provides a forum for sociologists concerned with the value-related aspects of sociological theory, research, and professional life. Seeks to extend the boundaries of humanist sociology by exploring connections between sociology and other disciplines.
Publications: *The Humanist Sociologist* newsletter, *Humanity and Society* journal
Training: Holds annual meeting
Job Listings: None

Association for the Sociology of Religion (ASR)

618 Southwest 2nd Avenue
Galva, IL 61434
sociologyofreligion.com
Members/Purpose: Works to encourage study and research in the sociology of religion and to promote the highest professional and scientific standards for research and publication in the sociology of religion.
Publications: *Sociology of Religion: A Quarterly Review*
Training: Holds annual meeting; sponsors research grants
Job Listings: None

Canadian Sociology and Anthropology Association (CSAA)

Concordia University
1455 de Maisonneuve West/Ouest
Montréal, QC H3G 1M8
csaa.ca

Members/Purpose: Promotes research, publication, and teaching in anthropology and sociology in Canada. Members include anthropologists and sociologists in education, government, and business, as well as students and those from other disciplines or affiliations who share a concern for anthropology and sociology.
Publications: *Canadian Review of Sociology and Anthropology, Society* newsletter.
Training: Sponsors annual conferences and other meetings
Job Listings: None

National Education Association (NEA)
1201 16th Street NW
Washington, DC 20036
nea.org
Members/Purpose: Professional organization and union of elementary and secondary school teachers, college and university professors, administrators, principals, counselors, and others concerned with education.
Publications: *NEA Today, Higher Education Advocate, NEA Handbook, NEA Almanac of Higher Education*
Training: Sponsors conferences
Job Listings: Offers job-seeking tips and helpful links

Population Association of America (PAA)
University of Maryland College Park
2112 Art-Sociology Building
College Park, MD 20742
popassoc.org
Members/Purpose: Professional society of individuals interested in demography and in its scientific aspects.
Publications: *Demography* (quarterly), directory of members, *PAA Affairs* online newsletter, *Applied Demography* newsletter, *Careers in Population*
Training: Holds annual meeting
Job Listings: Lists job announcements and funding opportunities online

Rural Sociological Society (RSS)
104 Gentry Hall
University of Missouri
Columbia, MO 65211
ruralsociology.org

Members/Purpose: Promotes the development of rural sociology through research, teaching, and extension work.

Publications: *The Rural Sociologists, Rural Sociology, Rural Realties* information series

Training: Holds annual meeting

Job Listings: Publishes employment opportunities online along with fellowship opportunities

6

Path 2:
Human Services

Community Organizations and Social Service Agencies

Thousands of nonprofit and government organizations serve the needs of the public. In fact, at most colleges and universities, you are certain to see web postings, notices on bulletin boards, and other announcements calling for volunteers to help staff local community organizations and social service agencies. Perhaps you have dedicated some of your free time to these organizations, such as by helping out with a mentoring program at the local public grade school or answering phones at the student crisis center. Even if your schedule hasn't allowed for it, as a sociology major you are probably already tuned in to the many causes and issues affecting the community. They must grab your attention because they so closely mirror the material you are studying. Indeed, your choice of sociology as a major may have grown out of your concern about the many social issues facing our communities and our nation at large.

Some of the issues that most frequently engage sociologists are manifested in these "real world" organizations. It's only logical that you would consider how you could explore these issues by seeking employment in an organization that serves the societal groups that you have studied. Consider the courses that you took in your degree program. They probably included topics such as:

Sociology of Mental Health
Aging and Society
Rural Sociology
Cultural Ecology
Criminology
Ethnicity

Social Deviance
The Family

This brief list of typical courses from the sociology major is a good place to start a job search relevant to the issues you studied.

You can forge a fascinating and challenging career in any of the thousands of human services agencies that segment society according to health, deviance, age, ethnicity, religion, and any number of other characteristics. While it may take a master's degree or higher to work as a professional sociologist, you can find a meaningful job as a working sociologist in many of these organizations. Such entry-level jobs can launch rich careers whether you stay in agency work for a lifetime or move on after a few years to acquire additional education.

Checking Out Social Agencies and Organizations

Put down this book for a moment and find the telephone directory. Look up "Social and Human Service Organizations." You'll find a significant number of listings, even in the slimmest of local directories. Many you'll recognize immediately, such as the American Red Cross or your state legal assistance fund. You'll also find a variety of local and state family planning groups, counseling offices, domestic violence shelters, and halfway houses. You may also notice additional agency names, which, though unfamiliar to you, you'll find intriguing. For example, your state may have an assistive technology and equipment center or a program of academic excellence to motivate inner-city youth. Other organizations are centered on issues such as helping people with AIDS, people with housing difficulties, or people in need of heating assistance. There will be programs offering abortion counseling or general counseling services for young people. Many agencies help people with disabilities.

If you look in a larger city or metropolitan directory or do a search on the Internet, you'll find a staggering number of human service agencies listed. You will be surprised at how narrowly focused some of the programs are. In fact, the headings may remind you of the chapters of your Introduction to Sociology text: Mental Health, Religion, Children's Services, Career Development Services, Senior Services, and similar headings.

You might also be astonished to see the sheer number of organizations listed under these particular headings. While you may be very interested in housing assistance issues, you may be surprised to see the large number of organizations listed under that heading. Each may have a very different mission. Some organizations may serve to organize residents, others may find housing for the homeless, others may repair and maintain the homes of the elderly who can no longer take care of their own houses and have limited incomes. Some organizations may use local youth to revitalize apartment buildings, providing them with meaningful work experience and housing at the same time.

These listings read like an index of our social concerns, our social structure, and our social conscience. In the needs they express and in the provision of an agency to help meet those needs, they are clear signs of society's response to these situations. It's fair to say that the size and breadth of these listings have as much to do with the size of the community as they do with the concern the community expresses for others and the determination of those committed to the public good to found organizations and agencies to help.

Typical Social Concerns

The choice of issues is indeed a rich one. Each organization presents its own set of issues. Community organizations and agencies for women present an excellent example. An organization may be information oriented, perhaps teaching about breast cancer detection or osteoporosis. It may be about role modeling, matching young women from disadvantaged homes with more mature women who can provide some friendship and support. It may be an activist group, seeking to end pay discrimination or sexual harassment in the workplace. One group's goal may be to offer support for women who have lost a child, husband, or companion. Another group may address sexual identity or gender role issues, such as groups for lesbians or transsexuals. The focus of women-oriented organizations is not exhausted by this short list.

Each group makes demands on the skills and talents of the workers serving them and challenges them to an ongoing development of their skills and talents. The following is a list of some social concerns, with capsule descriptions of relevant issues and statistics. An actual job description is included for each that indicates that a candidate with a sociology undergraduate degree would be welcomed.

Youth Concerns
Problems such as unemployment, dysfunctional families, and school systems that have difficulty coping contribute to a continuing delinquency problem

among young people. Issues such as crime, vandalism, drug and alcohol abuse, prostitution, early pregnancy, and gangs are covered widely in the media, making them prominent issues of social concern. For example, one of the most troubling developments is the astronomical rise in juvenile gangs. In the 1970s, nineteen states reported having gang problems, primarily in the larger cities. By 2000, every single state and the District of Columbia were reporting gang activity. In the twenty-first century, gangs are no longer limited to large cities. Whereas in the 1970s, the average population of a city with gangs was 182,000, today the average population of an affected city is under 40,000.

Our penal institutions are generally not very oriented toward or successful with rehabilitation. And many job-training programs have discovered the need for providing extensive follow-through for graduates to ensure employment. Working with juvenile offenders presents great challenges but also the possibility of large rewards for those working with them.

In addition, many young people are working hard to stay on track and need community organizations and other support systems to help them stay focused. After-school programs, counseling services, vocational training, sports, and recreation programs are appearing all over to satisfy this very real and positive need.

Poverty

Despite the wealth and resources of the United States, poverty remains a serious social issue, affecting millions of individuals and families. In 2006, the government's official poverty rate was $10,284 for an individual and $16,079 for a household of three, according to the U.S. Census bureau. The number of persons who were officially impoverished in 2006 was 36.5 million, representing more than 12 percent of the nation's population. Add to this the large number of the "working poor," wage earners whose income is perhaps above the official poverty rate but still inadequate to meet their families' needs. Homeless shelters in large cities must not only meet the needs of destitute individuals, but also provide shelter to families that have been forced from their homes.

Poverty is not the only problem. Alcoholism, drug abuse, illness, and a host of other social ills are also factors in chronic poverty, the treatment of which requires additional skills and knowledge on the part of the social service worker. The social service worker is not alone as an agent for change. Federal programs for jobs, housing, employment, and numerous preventative initiatives are available, as is an enormous network of other helping professionals.

Substance Abuse

Substance abuse remains a complex and challenging problem with a multitude of related issues. For the community and social service worker, addiction is a problem that requires the combined forces of both the medical community and helping professionals of social services. In the 2007 Monitoring the Future study, as reported by the White House Office of National Drug Control Policy, approximately 19 percent of eighth graders, 35 percent of tenth graders, and 47 percent of twelfth graders reported using illicit drugs at least once. According to the 2006 National Survey on Drug Use and Health, over 40 percent of women ages twelve or older reported using an illicit drug one or more times, and males reported even higher rates.

Along with the health and behavior problems involved, the substance abuse problem also carries severe economic repercussions. According to the Canadian Centre on Substance Abuse, the costs of substance abuse in Canada exceeds $40 billion annually, including legal substances such as tobacco and alcohol as well as a variety of illegal drugs. Society also pays a price in terms of the overall safety of our communities, as addiction often involves crime, particularly theft, to support the substance habit.

Drug and alcohol abuse destroys relationships, and rebuilding one's life from addiction is often a long, difficult journey. Self-help programs, halfway houses, and other services in a community provide vital therapies for the recovering addict.

Alcoholism. Alcoholism remains largely hidden to the majority of the public, but the community and social service worker is all too aware of the extent of alcoholism and the great sadness and pain it can bring to families, relationships, employers, and most importantly, to alcoholics themselves. It also contributes to lost productivity, including losses from alcohol-related illness, premature death, and crime. We are learning more about treatment methods, the effects on children of alcoholic parents, and the role heredity may play in the predisposition to alcoholism. Considerable work is being done on several frontiers for alcoholics and their problems, but it remains an enormous social challenge.

Crime

Crime is a real concern for every citizen. According to the U.S. Department of Justice, an estimated 1,417,745 violent crimes occurred nationwide in 2006. These incidents included aggravated assault, robbery, murder, and other crimes. In addition, there were an estimated 9,983,568 property crimes in the United States in 2006.

In Canada, even though crime rates tend to be lower, criminal activity is still a serious problem. According to Statistics Canada, 605 homicides were committed in 2006, along with 30,000 robberies, 250,000 break-ins, and 160,000 stolen vehicles.

Certainly, the destruction of lives and property remains a disturbing characteristic of our society. The price of justice is also high. At the end of 2006, the total number of individuals under the jurisdiction of federal or state adult correctional authorities was more than 2,258,000, according to the U.S. Bureau of Justice Statistics. In Canada, approximately 32,000 adults were incarcerated at any one time in 2005, with another 120,000 under supervision in the community, according to Statistics Canada. These populations present issues revolving around punishment versus rehabilitation in which community and social service workers are involved, some at prison sites, others assisting with reentry to the community.

Numerous citizen activist groups and agencies are appearing that self-police neighborhoods, crack down on drug activity in specific locales, or ensure housing projects are safe for residents. Organizers and coordinators help these groups in setting reasonable goals, raising funds, and focusing the efforts of volunteers to best achieve desired aims.

In this area, you'll probably work alongside criminologists. Criminology was an early offshoot of sociology that has now become its own discipline. Criminologists often have strong backgrounds in sociology. They help plan and direct juvenile and adult crime-prevention projects.

Mental Health

While public education has begun to remove the stigma associated with mental illness, much remains to be done to create an atmosphere of greater understanding and acceptance of people suffering from mental disorders. According to the National Institute of Mental Health, about one in four adults suffers from some type of diagnosable mental disorder in any given year. And it is estimated that 20 percent of Canadians will personally experience a mental illness in their lifetime, including disorders such as depression, bipolar disorder, schizophrenia, and anxiety disorders. The most serious disorders are experienced by about 6 percent of the population. Perhaps surprisingly, mental disorders are the leading cause of disability in the United States and Canada for persons between the ages of fifteen and forty-four.

In 2005, more than 32,000 people died from suicide in the United States, according to the National Center for Health Statistics, with another three thousand Canadians suffering the same fate, as documented by Statistics Canada. The vast majority, more than 90 percent, who killed themselves had a diagnosable mental disorder, such as depression. Similarly, the mortality rate among people with anorexia is a problem that is primarily affecting women. Over 3 percent of women suffer from anorexia during the course of their lifetimes. The mortality rate among people with anorexia has been estimated at 56 percent a year, which is about twelve times higher than the annual death rate due to all other causes of death among females age fifteen to twenty-four.

Mental illness exacts an enormous cost from the economy of the country, both in days missed at work and poor performance due to illness. Studies by the World Health Organization, the World Bank, and Harvard University have shown that mental illnesses, including suicide, account for more than 5 percent of the burden of disease in established market economies, which is more than the disease burden caused by all types of cancers. One positive result of increased public awareness is the increase in the numbers and types of treatment sites available.

Aging

One of the most significant developments is the aging of the American population. During the last decade of the twentieth century, the number of Americans sixty-five and older increased by 10.6 percent, compared to an increase of 9.1 percent for those under sixty-five. By 2006, approximately 12 percent of all Americans were sixty-five and over, according to the U.S. Census Bureau. And by 2050, they will make up about 21 percent of the U.S. population.

A similar pattern is emerging in Canada. According to Statistics Canada, the number of Canadians aged sixty-five and over increased by more than 446,700 from 2001 to 2006, representing nearly four times as many seniors as in the census of 1956.

This new generation of seniors is healthier, more active, and more interested in maintaining their activity level than ever before. They want city and town recreation programs to accommodate their needs, they use the YMCA and YWCA, and they belong to a number of activist organizations designed to lobby for their interests.

Though more physically active than their predecessors, with age comes an increased need for physical therapy, transportation services, counseling for depression and emotional difficulties, and help coping with necessary changes such as living situations and diet. Although some elderly individuals can afford to reside in planned communities, others live alone or in a variety of other settings. Some are in hospitals, nursing homes, or facilities that care for people with mental illnesses, including Alzheimer's disease.

Wide-Ranging Issues

This chapter has addressed only a few of the many social issues receiving the attention of social services organizations. Many other population groupings are served and issues are addressed. The listing of types of services that follows only scratches the surface of the possibilities available to the graduate looking to enter the community organization and social service field. Go down the list and think about which issues you are interested in. These are fields that can be emotionally as well as intellectually demanding, and each area is worth your exploration. Your local library or college career center can provide you with supplemental information. In addition, a number of professional organizations that can provide helpful information are listed at the end of this chapter.

Abortion alternatives counseling
Abortion counseling
Adoption services
Athletic services
Battered spouses' and children's services
Blind organizations and services
Charity services
Child counseling
Children's services
Chronic disease services
Communicable diseases counseling and services
Community services
Consumer services
Credit counseling
Crime victim services
Crisis intervention services
Day care assistance
Deaf and hearing impaired services
Developmentally disabled persons' services
Divorce counseling
Drug abuse and prevention services
Educational information services
Ethnic organizations and services
Family and individual services
Foster care services
Gay, lesbian, and bisexual organizations and services
Halfway houses

Health services
Home care services
Homeless persons' services
Housing assistance
Human services
Immigrant assistance
Legal counseling
Medical relief services
Mental health services
Men's services
Philanthropic services
Pregnancy counseling and prevention information
Pregnancy and maternity services
Rape crisis services
Religious organizations
Sex information and counseling
Single parents' services
Suicide prevention services
Tenants' services
Travelers' assistance
Vocational services
Volunteer services
Women's services
Youth services

Human Services and the Sociology Major

Clearly, there is a need for perceptive and sensitive employees who can bring their education in sociology to the table. The challenge for those who enter this field is to learn what these various organizations actually do. It's even more important to discover what roles are available for a sociology major with an undergraduate degree. For the sociology major interested in community and social service, the problem is not who will hire you or where you can work but how to choose among the many types of agencies that exist. Each is a world of specialized information, unique support networks, relationships with referral agencies, informational and financial resources, and dedicated professionals and paraprofessionals working to improve the human condition.

To best understand where you might fit in this jigsaw puzzle of agencies and organizations, it will help if you:

- Understand the goals and missions of social service work
- Realize your value to the service-agency labor pool
- Analyze the demands of actual job listings
- Consider your strengths relative to job demands

Social and community service connects people with the information and tools they need to cope with and surmount the challenges facing them. Community workers help to bring harmony to strained lives, enrich lives that may be impoverished in various respects, and teach people the skills and techniques to become capable of self-advocacy and self-sufficiency.

Any profession that deals with humans and the infinite number of issues they face from birth to death cannot be limited to workers of one educational preparation, one kind of knowledge, or one kind of experience. When issues as diverse as sexual abuse, disease, mental and physical disabilities, housing, insurance, education, crime, and alcoholism are part of the daily menu of problems presented to social service agencies, they obviously require an array of talents.

The field of community and social service draws from many academic backgrounds. The sociology major is an important resource. The fields of psychology, religion, counseling, medicine, health and nutrition, home economics, child care, law enforcement, political science, mental health, criminal justice, and, of course, social work also provide skilled workers. It is a networking, communicating, bridge-building, role-modeling, counseling, and mentoring partnership role that the social service worker plays in connecting clients with the many services and agencies providing assistance.

Definition of the Career Path

Looking at a current group of want ads for entry-level community and social service jobs, the skills and attributes they all require in common are the ability to

Meet immediate needs
Assess a wide range of conditions
Build a knowledge base
Keep accurate records
Provide counseling and referrals
Work with volunteers
Network and interact with multidisciplinary teams
Research and retrieve information

Because each job and each agency presents unique circumstances, the priorities of these job components vary with the position and the setting. Consider what your strengths are (refer to the self-assessment you completed in Part One) in determining how to choose the setting in which you may work most effectively.

Responding to Immediate Needs

In many situations, there are immediate and demanding needs to be met, such as shelter, food, and health care. Some clients can be assisted quickly, many others, very slowly. Sadly, many clients cannot be helped at all. Those who work in this field find that the rewards are found in reaching and assisting those clients who can be helped. Community organization and social service workers make a contribution each day by helping those who, if left alone, might not be able to do things for themselves.

> **Job posting in South Florida.** Dade County has openings for Social Workers in Child Welfare Services. MSW preferred. Culturally diverse population in a progressive, fast-paced setting. This is an excellent opportunity to join the next generation of practitioners and management.

Assessing Varying Conditions

The types of human conditions seen in various settings are described in the advertisements. You can expect to become quite adept at recognizing the signs of alcoholism, delirium tremens, diabetes, hypothermia, malnutrition, or addiction and will become skilled at assessing your client's self-help skills and willingness to change.

Understanding the Issues

In reading this, you no doubt have begun to appreciate the time and focus you need to bring to the job as an entry-level community organization or social service worker. All the while, as you improve your job performance (your ability to help), you will be acquiring valuable information, knowledge, and skills for working with the population you are serving. Your knowledge base will build almost imperceptibly, aided by in-service training, conferences, seminars, and a daily schedule of clients with their individual case histories. You will find your understanding of the system expanding, and the bureaucratic and legal aspects of assistance and support will become clearer and more workable. Laws and pending legislation can vary dramatically state by state, and even within states there can be differences in implementation. To be an effective community and social service agency worker, you must understand the system you are in and act as a guide in helping your client secure needed services. To do this well requires making contacts and connections, most often in the process of working with individual clients and learning how things work in your locality.

Though you provide helping skills yourself, much of your work depends on making connections with others and in advocating for your client the support and assistance he or she is eligible for. Understanding and learning that takes time and experience.

> **Social Work Assistant.** Our agency has an opening for a nursing home social work assistant, 40 hours per week. Experience and appropriate training preferred. Please send résumé. For more information on our facility, visit: xxx.net. To apply, submit résumé to the following address.

Maintaining Records

While all of this is going on, the community and social service worker must keep excellent records and may sometimes be responsible for determinations of financial assistance or other forms of aid. You may be called upon to explain local, state or provincial, or federal regulations or procedures to your clients and may actively assist them in their efforts to secure assistance.

Many new entrants into the field of social service are overwhelmed by the amount of paperwork and telephone work. Hours and hours of each day are spent chasing people down by telephone or processing paperwork. Carrying out administrative duties can certainly create doubts about the "service" in social and community service work.

Record keeping is a natural byproduct of the funding structure of many social service agencies, and it is probably best to realize now that many workers in this field spend their careers seeking the right balance between client services and administrative work.

Counseling

Counseling is a process of connection and deep human involvement between two people. Though there are many formal schools of counseling theory and technique, all counselors ultimately develop a counseling technique that works for them and for their clients. Often, for the clientele of the community and social service worker, the deeply empathic listening attention of the counselor is, in and of itself, therapeutic. Clients who have a caring listener who values them as individuals and to whom they can talk about their problems can be at the beginning of a road to healthier living.

Providing Referrals

Connecting clients to agencies and sources for everything from housing to day care is often a first step in the helping and rehabilitative process. Some clients need counseling and subsequent referral to drug-abuse or other treatment programs before other initiatives can successfully be undertaken.

An adult client with cerebral palsy may need help connecting with someone who can advocate for him finding appropriate and accessible housing. You may refer this same client to another agency that can provide help in wheelchair maintenance or physical therapy. The client may also need some assistance in applying for food stamps or in obtaining transportation to and from the store. Any given client may need referrals to a variety of support services.

The job involves interviewing clients to assess the scope and severity of their problems, to clarify their specific needs, and to determine how those needs might best be met. The community organization and social service agency worker then begins to organize all the necessary agencies, individuals, information, and resources to create some positive change.

Networking

As a new entrant in the field you are sure to build a network of contacts that you will be able to count on for help in serving your clients. This could take a variety of forms: solving a legal problem, finding long-term housing, or locating job-training programs, employment, and sources for food, clothing, or medical help. You will become very aware of the complexity of factors influencing every individual client's situation as well as the social fabric that contributes to their problems and the difficulties in solving them.

Research and Information Retrieval

The work of sociologists is intricately connected to that of many other professionals, including psychologists, physicians, economists, statisticians, urban and regional planners, political scientists, anthropologists, law enforcement and criminal justice officials, and social workers.

Sociologists and statisticians work together to analyze the significance of data. This research role is so important that it comprises one of the major career paths in this book (See Chapter 9: Path 5: Social Research and Data Analysis).

The results of sociological research have helped educators, lawmakers, administrators, and others interested in resolving social problems and formulating public policy. Some of the significant issues addressed by these sociologists include abortion rights, high school dropouts, homelessness, and latchkey children.

Though research may not be the dominant part of your job in human services work, you will certainly need to do it at some point in your job. Every day you'll encounter questions. "How many senior citizens live in town?" or "How many indigent poor are there in the state?" are typical of the simple inquiries that can have you working overtime if your research skills are rusty.

Many larger human service agencies have research departments that hold job prospects for the new sociology graduate. For example, health sociologists have done dramatic research work on the AIDS virus and were part of the research team at the Centers for Disease Control in Atlanta that discovered the first cluster of sexually transmitted cases of AIDS.

Sociology in Social Work

For many jobs, you will be competing with social work graduates for the same position. You may already have encountered some confusion among your friends or relatives who think you are getting a social work degree. The explanation of the relationship between the two will be instructive to you as you build confidence for the job search.

Sociology forms the body of knowledge that the social action of social work is founded upon. Both fields are deeply concerned with certain values that are embedded in the culture. Social work is interested in this body of knowledge and theory only insofar as the discovery and interpretation of those facts allow it to assist in doing something about the social problems of individuals and groups.

As a newly graduated sociology major, it's only natural to look at those jobs where you can direct your learning toward results-oriented outcomes—the fields of social services. As you progress in your career, and if you happen to add to your education, you may want to return to the field of sociological theory and research.

The job listings in this chapter should give you some sense of the diversity of work present in social services, not only in the kinds of activities social service workers engage in, but also in the kinds of problems that affect the people they work with and the age and gender mix of those populations. The breadth and scope of social service work through an agency or community organization and its initiatives results in an equally broad scope in the selection of candidates for social service jobs.

What you took special notice of were the fairly generalized degree demands: in most cases, a bachelor's degree or a sociology degree or some reasonably related degree. Most employers, for obvious reasons, would prefer previous experience so that job candidates understand the job and the issues of the people they will be working with.

While the generalized requirements may please some, others may be skeptical. Why don't they demand a social work degree? How can they be so loose in job qualifications when the work is so important? The answers lie in the nature of social service work. It is enormously demanding—many would say taxing—of the social service worker's energy, patience, time, and physical resources. Although the field has an incredibly wide range of pay for similar jobs, depending upon the employment setting, high salaries have not been a tradition of the community and social service field. Thus, the short answer may be that hiring officials who fill tough jobs paying less than top wages must draw from a wide pool of applicants.

There's another equally valid reason. When you look at the spectrum of problems social service workers must wrestle with and the diversity of the human beings who are placed before them, it is difficult to know where the talent may lie to help alleviate some of the struggle. Certainly, we have social workers who have studied the issues and earned a degree in the subject on the bachelor's, master's, and doctoral level. Others come to these same issues and concerns with a different yet equally valuable preparation in their academic areas and life experiences.

A wonderful book, now sadly out of print but still available in academic libraries, is *Sociology in Social Work* by Peter Leonard from the University of Liverpool. He explains the natural and vital relationship between sociology and social work and offers his outlook on the future of the relationship and the use of sociological knowledge in social work.

Professional and Personal Growth Opportunities

If you are seriously contemplating a career in community and social services, you have probably asked yourself whether you will be able to sustain a life-long career in this field. Perhaps you are worried about burning out, becoming overwhelmed by the magnitude of the social problems facing so many people. Will you become less effective as you continue in this field, becoming disinterested or hardened when faced with a particular set of problems, or simply not being able to handle the deluge of individuals seeking your assistance?

As you begin your career, you can do three specific things that will help you successfully deal with these issues over time. First of all, think about whether the skills you are using and the knowledge base you are building can be transferred to other populations and settings. Second, think about preparing for advancement. And third, take care of your own needs.

Transferring Your Skills and Knowledge

One way to prevent burnout is to change your work setting from time to time. Successful changes happen as a result of being aware of which skills and knowledge are valued in a given workplace. Some of the skills and knowledge you acquire as you begin your career will be directly transferable to different situations, while other skills and knowledge will not relate as well to other settings. Look for the common threads! A position assisting homeless adults will provide some good experience in working with an older population, and that work can relate to a number of other, more stable, eldercare situations. Work in adult substance abuse might prove a good basis for a move to an adolescent substance abuse clinic. However, a move from a facility servicing homeless adults to a residential center caring for child victims of sexual or physical abuse would be more difficult to make. Both the type of facility and the type of client would have changed, so fewer skills and less knowledge would transfer.

Preparing for Advancement

You can advance in community and social service work by building upon your knowledge base and helping skills. That, by necessity, suggests working with a particular population and learning the resources that exist for that group until you are proficient. Job growth might then come in the form of more supervisory responsibility for other caregivers, management control of a facility, or advanced or specialized education in your field.

Seeing to Your Own Needs

It's no mystery why community and social service workers burn out. It's a tough, tough job, and some professionals simply get weary of the obstacles put in their clients' way or the backsliding that occurs among people they have strived to help.

You may get tired, you may get cynical, or you may want a job that is less physically and emotionally draining. Changing the population you work with is certainly one technique, especially if many of the issues are familiar to you. Growing within your specialty and taking an administrative or management position is another option.

Whatever you decide to do, however, make it an active choice. Don't let your career just "happen." You don't want your boss to take you aside one day and suggest that you're overextended, tired, and no longer effective. Take your own career pulse from time to time, and ask yourself how you truly feel about the work you are engaged in. If you feel you need something different, make it your choice. Community and social service is a noble calling with rich rewards, but it makes equally insistent demands on your time and energy.

The Working Environment

Community organization and social service agency employees at every level of expertise (doctoral, master's, bachelor's, and paraprofessional) are employed in a number of different settings. The setting, in large part, dictates the types of activities in which social service workers are engaged, the jobs and duties they have, the types of clients and client needs they will encounter, and the ways in which they will practice their social service profession.

Some specific issues to consider include

- Population served
- Source of funding for agency/service
- Working hours
- Specific issues of the clientele
- Personal safety

Population Served

Many agencies serve specific age populations, so if you feel the age of your clientele is an important condition, be sure to target the appropriate agencies. Some services are structured for particular age groups, so activities, programs, and atmosphere all combine to say to the client "This is a for-you service." The Elderhostel program is a fine example of an organization that responds to active seniors who want learning to be lifelong and who retain a curiosity and enthusiasm about the world around them. Shelters for adolescent males or after-school drop-in counseling centers are other good examples of age-targeted programs. Other services are age blind and are built around a health condition (osteoporosis), disease entity (AIDS), physical activity (swimming), and so forth.

Agency Funding Considerations

The stability of funding is an important consideration for any helping service. Funds that are not stable, that perhaps need to be renewed each year, can create a sense of impermanence, affect staff morale, and delay the timely delivery of services.

Other agencies may have relatively stable funding but require significant development work to continually raise money. You will be called upon to assist in fund-raising efforts in these circumstances. While necessary to continued viability, this fund-raising work can often be an additional burden on already overworked staff.

Some grant-funded programs ultimately end, or program funding slowly drops and programs are disbanded, leaving workers to seek new employment. Funding sources can also affect the physical facilities, location, supplies, services, and quality of staff of the organization.

Working Hours

Community and social service jobs differ from some other jobs because of the hours. Service providers work many different shifts and schedules, especially in the areas of homelessness, drug and substance abuse, and sheltered care.

You may have standard rotating eight-hour shifts, or you may have three full days on and four days off. You may have sleep-in accommodations but need to be available twenty-four hours. There are also the more traditional thirty-seven- to forty-hour workweeks. You'll need to consider this aspect of your work carefully and think about how various jobs will affect your personal life, your relationships, your outside interests, and your overall well-being.

Dealing with Client Issues

Some substance abusers steal to support their habits. Adolescent men and women have unprotected sex before marriage. The list of problems and behaviors goes on and on. These behaviors are probably inconsistent with your own values and behavior.

But your clients need help, not judgment. It is important for you, as you explore possible work settings, to ascertain how you feel about the issues of the people you work with. Compassion, caring, a sense of humor, and hopefulness are what your clients need, not lecturing, censorship, or condemnation. You need to consider this as you explore various jobs. With which kinds of issues and clients will you be able to work most effectively?

Personal Safety

When people encounter hardships and struggles in their lives, it can have pronounced effects on their temperaments. Anger, hostility, and violence may lie close to the surface, and from time to time, there are threats to the personal safety of community and social service workers.

Most professionals would assure you this is not a dominant concern in their workday lives. They exercise caution in their client relationships, they share their concerns with coworkers, and they activate response systems, including the police, if threats occur. In some settings, such as abortion clinics, overnight shelters, or disaster-relief situations, tempers flare and outbreaks of violence may occur. In most cases, personnel have been trained to deal with this and are able to act effectively to minimize the risk of danger to all involved.

Think about your own ability to tolerate conflict and mediate possible violence. Consider your personal, physical characteristics and the population you are interested in serving. It's also a good idea to talk to professionals working in these areas for greater insight into issues of physical safety in their jobs. There is no better way to find out the real story behind a career than to talk with people who are already engaged in the profession. Talking to people in the field will provide a reality check that no amount of reading can give you.

The Right Qualifications

Social service and community work is so diverse that it would be foolish to try to create a comprehensive list or menu of necessary personal characteristics. The long list that follows suggests many of the personal characteristics that people in this profession draw upon to some extent or another. The counseling techniques that may be effective in establishing rapport with young, unwed mothers may not serve the social service worker as well when dealing with the chronically mentally ill. But many of these qualities are helpful across the board in a variety of social and community service positions. If you are considering a career in community and social service, you will need to review this list and rate yourself on these criteria.

Maturity
Concern for others
Responsibility
High standards
Sense of humor
Good with people
Dedication
Speaking skills
Discretion
Objectivity
Independence
Stability
Empathy
Resilience
Communication
Teaching
Idealism
Ethics
Sensitivity
Mutual respect
Listening skills
Productivity
Realism
Innovation
Writing
Thoughtfulness
Responsiveness

Concern for Others

To engage the client and to assess the situation, the social service worker needs empathy, sensitivity, and an ability to establish and maintain rapport. You also need to appreciate the wonderful diversity present among people.

Working with frustrated adolescents may require talking with them for quite a while before they begin to open up and talk to you about their problems. Elderly patients, for example, may share their fears and concerns more easily if you begin by letting them show you a family album or some favorite pictures.

Appropriate Detachment

To be effective, however, you will need to rely on your maturity and ability to remain removed (or detached) from the client's problems. The community and social service professional will find no paucity of clients and many problems to deal with that can seem almost insurmountable. The work goes on and on, and sometimes progress is very slow.

For that reason, you need to pace yourself. You need to respect your own limitations and what you can accomplish. If you are exhausted or over-wrought or allow clients to call you at home or interfere with your personal life, you will eventually self-extinguish. What help can you be to the system if you are burned out?

True professionals know their limitations and understand the importance of leaving work at work. They appreciate their own needs for rejuvenation and restoration each day to be able to return and do effective work. Clients may have problems you can help with, but you must continually remind yourself that the client's problems are not your problems.

Working the System

Workers in human service agencies must be quick studies in political systems to be able to marshal the necessary resources to help solve clients' problems. Referral networks and sources of financial aid and housing entitlements all have their hierarchies, paperwork, and influential personalities. To do your best for your clients is to understand not only how the system should work, but how it, in fact, does work.

Flexibility

Flexibility is another key personal trait needed in community and social service work. Work hours or shifts may change constantly, the physical location where you carry out your duties may move, and even the members of your team may constantly change because of different schedule rotations. Assess your ability to be happy with the level of flexibility required in the positions you are considering.

Professional Qualifications

There are both preprofessional and professional positions in community and social service work, largely determined by degree level and type. Preprofessional positions are those nondegree or associate-degree positions in which job holders act as aides or assistants to social and community service workers. Professional positions are those in which the individual has at least a bachelor's degree in sociology, social work, psychology, or some other human service field that will satisfy the social service agencies.

Licensure/Certification. Workers in the community and social services field have come under increasing public scrutiny. As in any area of human endeavor, there have been scandals and examples of unethical behavior. Laws and regulations surrounding the provision for services have increased exponentially, and many professional organizations publish detailed ethical guidelines for their members.

In addition to advanced degree attainment as an outward mark of professionalism, many states and provinces will require you to have licenses and/or certification to do some types of work. Licensure is the process by which states and provinces ensure that you have attained certain educational and/or experiential standards, often involving some type of written examination. These standards help the public know the individual has met some state-mandated criterion for professionalism. Licensing boards also have the authority to discipline unethical or fraudulent practitioners by revoking their licenses.

Certification through professional organizations promotes standards of education, practice, accountability, discretion, ethics, and visibility. Certification can involve testing or the documentation of professional development and years of practice. It is often issued for a limited period of time.

Certification by the Sociological Practice Association (SPA) is required for some positions in clinical sociology and applied sociology, especially at the doctoral level.

See your career office or talk with state or provincial officials for information on licensure and your applicable professional associations for certification information.

Knowledge of Other Languages. Because of the expanding immigrant communities in our cities, urban metropolitan job announcements in social and community service will often express the desire for fluency in Spanish, Chinese, Vietnamese, Cambodian, or another language. While the record of assimilation, especially in language acquisition, among these new citizens is remarkable, new arrivals and the elderly often cannot be effectively served without being able to communicate in their native tongues.

Earnings

According to the U.S. Department of Labor, median annual earnings of social and human service assistants were $25,580 in 2006. The top 10 percent earned more than $40,780, while the lowest 10 percent earned less than $16,180. In typical areas of employment, median salaries were $30,510 in local government, $24,490 in individual and family services, and $22,530 in vocational rehabilitation services.

For social workers, median annual earnings were $37,480 in 2006. The lowest 10 percent earned less than $24,480, and the top 10 percent earned more than $62,530. In industries employing large numbers of social workers, median pay in elementary and secondary schools was $48,360; in local government, $43,500; and in individual and family services, $32,680. Median annual earnings of medical and public health social workers were $43,040 in 2006, while mental health and substance abuse social workers earned $35,410.

In Canada, social workers averaged C$51,418 in 2007, and community and social service workers had average incomes of C$33,467.

Earning for these and other types of positions in human services may be influenced by a number of factors, including the size and type of employer, the geographic region, and your own experience and credentials. If any of these figures are lower than you anticipated, be sure to complete the "Calculate Your Economic Needs" portion of the self-assessment in Part One to verify that you will be able to meet your basic economic needs.

Career Outlook

According to U.S. Department of Labor projections, employment of social and human service assistants is expected to grow by nearly 34 percent through 2016. Job prospects are expected to be especially good for applicants with college-level training. Overall demand for social and human services is expected to continue growing in the foreseeable future, as the general population grows and the number of elderly who need services such as support during medical crises, adult day care, meal delivery programs, and other assistance increases.

Demand will also be strong for workers who are qualified to help persons of all ages who are homeless, mentally disabled, or who have problems with drug or alcohol abuse. Potential employers include private social service agencies; state, provincial, and local governments; and other organizations that provide social or human services.

Employment for social workers is also expected to grow much faster than the average for all occupations through 2016, especially for those who specialize in working with senior citizens or who work in rural areas. The U.S. Department of Labor projects that employment of social workers will increase by more than 20 percent through 2016. As with social and human service assistants, population increases and the growing elderly population will create greater demand for trained social workers, as will demands for other types of assistance in the broad-based area of social and human services.

Strategy for Finding the Jobs

It's never too early to begin your job search. What's more, much of the quest to land the right job in human services can be started even before you've finished your class work and polished your résumé. Here are six tasks you can undertake to enhance your job search:

1. Determine which community and social concerns interest you the most.
2. Identify your own personal qualifications.
3. Familiarize yourself with the required professional qualifications.
4. Build skills and gain direct experience with the population you want to focus on.
5. Network with professionals working in the field.
6. Relate your sociology background to what the employer needs.

Undertaking these activities, together with the other phases of the job search outlined in Part One of this book, will put you on the right track as you begin to establish your career and make the most of your sociology degree.

Potential Employers

You have an enormous variety of options when it comes to potential employers. You might want to begin your investigations by looking into these groupings:

- Nonprofit agencies
- Medical and health organizations
- Federal/state/provincial/local governmental agencies
- Corrections and rehabilitation
- Insurance companies

Exploring the different types of employment opportunities will bring you that much closer to discovering the best fit for your career goals.

Nonprofit Agencies
Nonprofit agencies offer an incredibly wide array of community and social services, and each hires workers to provide, oversee, administer, and manage these services. They need you, the sociology major, on their staffs. Whether

you're working in consumer services, aid to the homeless, or immigration assistance, your skills in counseling, record keeping, and referral will be critical to your success.

Help in Locating These Employers. There are several publications and websites that help you locate job openings in the nonprofit world. These include the *Chronicle of Philanthropy* (philanthropy.com) and the *Non-Profit Times* (npt.com). General job sites such as Monster (monster.com) list jobs with nonprofits. Be sure to check the sites of individual organizations as well. Another helpful resource is *Government Job Finder: Where the Jobs Are in Local, State, and Federal Government,* by Daniel Lauber (Planning Communications, 2008).

Medical/Health Organizations

These types of facilities serve a range of clients and assist them with such issues as alcohol and chemical dependency, rape, family planning, hospice care, health, and AIDS. The knowledge and skills you've built could be put to use in any of these settings. If, for instance, you were an AIDS outreach worker and your clients were deaf Americans, you would use your specialized knowledge in working with this type of client to educate them about the disease and help them receive available media as well as other services.

Help in Locating These Employers. Be sure to look at the *AHA Guide to U.S. Hospitals, Health Care Systems, Networks, Alliances, Health Organizations, Agencies, & Providers* (American Hospital Association, 2008). Also check out the sites of individual health care organizations, as well as general job sites such as HotJobs (hotjobs.com).

Governmental Agencies

About one-quarter of what the U.S. Department of Labor calls human services workers, which includes some community and social service workers, are employed by state, provincial, and local governments in hospitals and outpatient mental health centers; in departments of human services (mental health divisions); and in facilities for people with mental retardation and developmental disabilities.

The diversity of possible employment roles and situations is considerable in this category. Providing counseling to the families of enlisted military personnel, doing in-home visits for the infirm elderly to ensure service provision, case managing in a mental health facility, and coordinating educational benefits for women on welfare are just a few of the possibilities.

Help in Locating These Employers. Two resources to start with are *The Book of U.S. Government Jobs: Where They Are, What's Available & How to Get One*, by Dennis Damp (Bookhaven Press, 2008) and *Government Job Finder: Where the Jobs Are in Local, State, and Federal Government*, by Daniel Lauber (Planning Communications, 2008). They provide helpful specifics about weaving your way through the maze of public employment. Be sure to also review actual government job listings posted at usajobs.gov or at govjobs.ca.

Corrections and Rehabilitation (Federal, State, or Provincial Local)

Social service workers in corrections and rehabilitation at all governmental levels may have job titles such as child welfare caseworker, clinical psychologist, corrections counselor, parole officer, recreation leader, or social group worker. Sociology majors who have taken related course work or have an academic minor in a field such as criminal justice and have also gained direct work experience (internship, part-time job, summer job, volunteer work) are eligible for many of these types of positions.

Help in Locating These Employers. To get started, be sure to network with authorities in the relevant state, provincial, and local agencies to get the latest information on hiring needs and employment application procedures. The U.S. Department of Justice has information regarding careers in this field on their website, usdoj.gov. Also check the websites of state, provincial, or local agencies.

Insurance Companies

Many health insurers provide managed health care services to their members, and they employ sociology majors to fill positions in customer service, claims, and provider relations. You probably won't meet your clients face to face, but you will assist them in obtaining the physical and mental health services they are entitled to.

For a large employee benefit program, you might serve as a telemarketing resource, using computerized directory information to provide referrals to individuals seeking assistance. This is a sophisticated position, requiring excellent listening and questioning skills to determine need as well as critical thinking skills to determine a number of appropriate treatment options.

Help in Locating These Employers. Sites such as Monster (monster.com) and HotJobs (hotjobs.com) provide numerous job listings within the insurance industry. Also check with professional associations and major insurance companies. For the latter, look over their websites and then contact the human resources department at those companies where you believe you might want to work to determine their application procedures.

Possible Job Titles

You will see a wide variety of job titles associated with community and social services. Sometimes the word *counselor* is in the job title, which oftentimes indicates an entry-level position. For workers who have more experience through part-time or summer employment or an internship, the term *coordinator* might be used. More experienced workers who have case management experience or who are responsible for supervision of other workers, facilities, or budgets will often have the term *manager, director,* or *supervisor* in their job title. Review the titles shown below and look for job listings that match your level of experience.

Care manager
Case worker
Child care worker
City manager
Community services specialist
Community support clinician
Consultant
Counseling coordinator
Criminologist
Demographer
Educator
Environmental organizer
Family counselor
Fund-raising assistant director
Gerontologist
Historian
Hospital administrator
Housing coordinator
Labor relations specialist
Medical records worker
Mental retardation and mental health counselor
Occupational career counselor

Parent counselor/educator
Prevention counselor
Program coordinator
Program director
Program manager
Project manager
Public administrator
Public assistance worker
Public health supervisor
Public relations manager
Recreation worker
Research assistant
Rural health outreach worker
Social worker
Substance abuse counselor
Survey worker
Women's counselor
Youth specialist

Professional Associations

Because community and social service work takes place in a variety of settings, just an introduction to a variety of possible professional associations is provided here. Contact those that have titles or work with populations you are interested in. *The Encyclopedia of Associations* and other references cited provide additional information about the goals and activities of these associations.

American Association of the Deaf-Blind (AADB)
8630 Fenton Street, Suite 121
Silver Spring, MD 20910-3803
aadb.org
Mission/Purpose: Operates as a national consumer organization serving deaf-blind Americans and their supporters. Members include deaf-blind people from diverse backgrounds as well as family members, professionals, interpreters, and other interested supporters.
Publications: *The Deaf-Blind American, AADB E-News*, brochures, fact sheets, and white papers
Training: Sponsors national conferences and other meetings
Job Listings: None

**American Association on Intellectual and
Developmental Disabilities (AAIDD)**
444 North Capitol Street NW, Suite 846
Washington, DC 20001-1512
aaidd.org
Members/Purpose: Promotes progressive policies, sound research, effective
practices, and universal human rights for people with intellectual and
developmental disabilities.
Publications: *American Journal on Mental Retardation, Intellectual &
Developmental Disabilities, AAIDD F.Y.I.* electronic newsletter, and
AJMR and IDD abstracts
Training: Annual conventions and other meetings, including Training
Institutes
Job Listings: None

**American Public Human Services
Association (APHSA)**
810 First Street NE, Suite 500
Washington, DC 20002
aphsa.org
Members/Purpose: Serves state and local human service agencies and
individuals who work in or are interested in public human service
programs. Develops and promotes policies and practices that improve
the health and well-being of families, children, and adults.
Publications: *Annual Public Human Services Directory, Policy & Practice*
magazine, *This Week in Washington, This Week in Health, Medicaid
Monthly*
Training: Offers a variety of conferences and training opportunities
Job Listings: Offers online job bank

American School Health Association (ASHA)
7263 State Route 43
P.O. Box 708
Kent, OH 44240
ashaweb.org
Members/Purpose: Promotes comprehensive and constructive school
health programs, including the teaching of health, health services, and a
healthful school environment.
Training: Holds conferences
Publications: *Health in Action, Journal of School Health*
Job Listings: None

American Society of Criminology (ASC)
1314 Kinnear Road, Suite 212
Columbus, OH 43212-1156
asc41.com
Members/Purpose: Embraces scholarly, scientific, and professional knowledge concerning the etiology, prevention, control, and treatment of crime and delinquency. Focuses on measurement and detection of crime, review of legislation and the practice of law, and examination of the law enforcement, judicial, and correctional systems.
Publications: *Criminology, Criminology & Public Policy, The Criminologist* newsletter
Training: Holds annual meeting
Job Listings: Sponsors employment exchanges at annual meetings; lists employment openings online

Association of Academic Health Centers (AAHC)
1400 Sixteenth Street NW, Suite 720
Washington, DC 20036
aahcdc.org
Members/Purpose: Chief administrative officers of university-based health centers in the United States. Interdisciplinary in focus, with a primary interest in total health education.
Training: Leadership institute and other education programs
Publications: Directory, annual report
Job Listings: None

Canadian College of Health Service Executives (CCHSE)
292 Somerset Street West
Ottawa, ON K2P 0J6
ccshe.org
Members/Purpose: Serves three thousand individual and seventy-five corporate members working in all health sectors across Canada. Provides a forum for exchanging information and best practices, and sponsors a variety of professional development resources and opportunities.
Training: Holds National Healthcare Leadership Conference and other meetings; sponsors certification program
Publications: Annual report, *Healthcare Management FORUM*, position papers
Job Listings: Publishes job openings online

Canadian Mental Health Association (CMHA)
Phenix Professional Building
595 Montreal Road, Suite 303
Ottawa, ON K1K 4L2
cmha.ca
Members/Purpose: Serves more than one hundred thousand Canadians in promoting the mental health of all and supporting the resilience and recovery of people experiencing mental illness.
Publications: Mental health pamphlet series, research reports, annual reports
Training: Holds annual conference and other meetings; offers online continuing education opportunities
Job Listings: None

Canadian Sociological Association
Concordia University
SB-323
1455 de Maisonneuve West
Montréal, QC H3G 1M8
csaa.ca
Members/Purpose: Promotes research, publication, and teaching of sociology in Canada.
Publications: *Canadian Review of Sociology and Anthropology, Society* newsletter
Training: Holds annual conferences and other meetings
Job listings: Offers online job listings

Learning Disabilities Association of Canada (LDAC)
250 City Centre Avenue,
  Suite 616
Ottawa, ON K1R 6K7
ldac-taac.ca
Members/Purpose: Represents a network of ten provincial and two territorial learning disabilities associations with more than seven thousand members across Canada. Advocates for policies to protect and strengthen rights and opportunities of individuals with learning disabilities.
Publications: *NATIONAL* newsletter; various manuals, guides, and self-help and reference books

Training: Holds workshops, national conferences, and provincial/territorial conferences
Job Listings: None

Medical Group Management Association (MGMA)

104 Inverness Terrace East
Englewood, CO 80112-5306
mgma.com
Members/Purpose: Serves medical practice managers and others interested in the area of medical practice management.
Training: Offers a certification program; sponsors conferences, webcasts, and other professional development opportunities
Publications: *MGMA Connexion* magazine, member directory
Job Listings: Offers MGMA Career Center, which includes online job postings

National Organization for Human Services (NOHS)

Metropolitan State College of Denver
Campus Box 8, P.O. Box 173362
Denver, CO 80217
nationalhumanservices.org
Members/Purpose: Strives to promote excellence in human service delivery in an increasingly complex world. Addresses social, behavioral, and educational issues in society; focuses on improvements in direct service, public education, program development, planning and evaluation, administration, and public policy.
Publications: *The Link* newsletter, *Human Service Education* journal
Training: Sponsors conferences, special events, and online information resources
Job Listings: Offers online career center

National Rural Health Association (NRHA)

521 East 63rd Street
Kansas City, MO 64110
nrharural.org
Members/Purpose: Purpose is to create a better understanding of health care problems unique to rural areas, utilize a collective approach in finding positive solutions, articulate and represent the health care needs of rural America, and supply current information to rural health care programs throughout the country.

Training: Offers continuing education credits for medical, dental, nursing, and management courses
Publications: *Journal of Rural Health, Rural Roads, Rural Clinician Quarterly, NHRA e-News*
Job Listings: Offers online career center

Society for Healthcare Strategy and Market Development (SHSMD)
c/o American Hospital Association
One North Franklin Street, 28th Floor
Chicago, IL 60606
shsmd.org
Members/Purpose: Persons employed or active in hospitals, hospital councils or associations, hospital-related schools, and health care organizations responsible for marketing and public relations.
Training: Offers conferences, seminars, webcasts, and other professional development opportunities
Publications: *AHA News Now, e-Connect, Inside HSMD, Spectrum*
Job Listings: Offers online "Career Link"

Society for Social Work and Research (SSWR)
11240 Waples Mill Road, Suite 200
Fairfax, VA 22030
sswr.org
Members/Purpose: Promotes the advancement of social work research. Works collaboratively with other organizations that are committed to improving support for research among social workers. Members include faculty members in schools of social work and other professional schools, research staff in public and private agencies, and graduate students. Members come from the United States and Canada as well as Australia and other nations, representing more than two hundred universities and institutions.
Publications: *SSWR* newsletter, *Research on Social Work Practice, Social Service Review*
Job Listings: Offers electronic job posting service

7

Path 3:
Human Resources
Management

Human resources management? A job path for a sociology major?
This may be your initial reaction on considering the title of this chapter. But don't be surprised. As a sociology major, you've studied human society and social behavior in groups and institutions. You've analyzed how individuals adapt to a wide range of situations and how groups of individuals coalesce to form social units. And perhaps you have also worked part-time and had a chance to observe firsthand how some of the theories play out in a real-world environment.

Sociology is actually quite relevant to the human resources management function of many organizations. Human resources is the department that most often brings people into the institution when they are hired. It is where people often seek job growth, training, or conflict resolution. And it is the department most often given the task of managing workplace change. These issues and how workers react to them are central to the concerns of sociologists.

You are probably well aware of the difficulties that often arise in today's workplace. With a little reflection, you can see the implications for human resources staff. In times of recession, human resources professionals are very often responsible for handling the layoffs and terminations; on the bright side, when the economy improves, they make certain that the right people are found for various positions. Despite progress, episodes of discrimination based on gender, race, sexual orientation, and other factors still occur. As the population of our country becomes even more heterogeneous, human resources professionals must build organizations from an increasingly diverse population. There are corresponding challenges to assimilation, inclusion, and tolerance. Human resources professionals try to create understanding and, hopefully, appreciation and enjoyment of this diversity.

Reading the newspaper or web-based news reports should also make you aware of the large number of lawsuits between employers and employees. Issues of harassment, discrimination, illegal firing and layoffs, and workplace injury or stress have escalated exponentially in recent years and have resulted in additional challenges for those working in the human resources area. Each lawsuit puts a special burden on human resources departments. Parties in a lawsuit may request documentation that includes personnel files, records of vacation or sick days, training opportunities, formal commendations or reprimands, and many other kinds of data from the human resources department. Recently, historical e-mail files have also come under scrutiny as a possible source of documentation. These requests can add a tremendous burden to an already busy office.

Potential employees are more aggressively interested in the economic health of their employers. They are concerned, too, about the possibility of being fired or laid off. Employees are not so naïve as to think they will be with the same firm for all of their lives. They also recognize the possibility that the organization may be bought or move or even fail. Many of them want to know from human resources what contingency plans are in effect in any of these situations. Will there be severance pay, outplacement services, counseling, relocation assistance, or transfers to a branch office?

The possibility of job loss and/or frequent job changes (something many trend analysts feel is the new reality for employees) means workers will be more aggressive in extracting not only benefits but also training and development from current employers. Employees as a group may demand resource acquisitions (gym or weight room, diet counseling, blood pressure checks, ergonomic consultations) and an accounting from the organization's management on money spent on staff development. As workers realize that they must always be ready to acquire new skills in preparation for new jobs, they will be more aggressive in using every benefit opportunity. Employees' use of benefits increases the work of human resources as well as the cost to the organization. Later in this chapter, when working conditions are described, you will find an expanded discussion of the training and development role human resources professionals must play.

Health care issues often dominate the news, and as the United States moves slowly toward more comprehensive health care, there will be a dramatic effect on employers and employees. Workers who previously could not leave their jobs for fear of jeopardizing health benefits because of their own or a family member's preexisting condition will now be assured coverage. Part-time workers will not necessarily lose coverage under new plans. These changes may indicate that we will see greater worker mobility and less loyalty than in the past, as employees are not tied by benefits to a particular employer. Since out-processing a former employee and in-processing and training new talent is costly, human resources professionals have much to be concerned about if worker mobility is no longer tied to health benefits.

Organizations are subtly affected in a positive way by the core of long-term employees who have some history with the organization and have learned to work together as a team. If that team breaks up beyond a critical point, some of that efficiency and networking will be lost, and that hurts the organization's ability to function as effectively.

Definition of the Career Path

"Human resources" is an apt description, since this area of the organization manages the resources of human productivity for the organization. Sociology could be an excellent preparation for a career in this area if you understand how you will use your degree in a human resources job.

If you are still working toward your degree, take every opportunity to add elective courses that would be most relevant to a human resources function. These include courses such as Sociologists at Work, Introduction to General Psychology, Methods of Social Research, Applied Sociology, and Aging and Society. The anthropology courses in a combined anthropology/ sociology degree program would not hold as much relevance for a career in human resources, but the workplace as a social organization would be directly reflected in your sociology courses. A few courses normally taken by business majors, such as Introduction to Management or Human Resources Management, can also be helpful.

If you've already graduated, your academic program in sociology has also helped you build a critical set of transferable skills that are highly valued in human resources. You mastered them in the context of studying sociology, but now you must make them relevant to the human resources employer. These skills include your ability to analyze, evaluate, draw conclusions, interview, manage time, write, manage projects, master computer technology, and plan. Each of these skills is critical to functioning effectively in human resources.

The Human Resources Department

What is it like to work in the human resources area? A look at the overall mission of a human resources department can be revealing, along with ways the mission affects the activities of the department.

Major human resources functions include the following:

- Hiring and placement
- Salary administration
- Employee benefits administration
- Training and development
- Data management

Hiring and Placement

Ideally, healthy organizations assimilate new employees in a way that enhances productivity. One of the primary tasks of the human resources department is to help bring new workers into a company as others retire, change jobs, get promoted, or move away.

In most organizations, the ultimate hiring decision is made by the department needing staff. Those within a department are best equipped to judge whether a candidate is qualified for the job they seek to fill. Human resources departments, however, often serve as gateways to the departments: collecting applications, assembling the candidates' files, and performing credential checks and background investigations. They might conduct training workshops for supervisors and their staff on how to conduct interviews fairly and objectively. Except in situations where the demand for lower-level employees is heavy, the human resources department seldom makes hiring decisions, except for a human resources employee.

It is a different matter, however, once an employee is hired. A common responsibility of the human resources departments is to provide new employee orientation. This may include a tour of the employer's facility and will surely include a lengthy discussion of rules and regulations, policies and procedures, benefits and compensation. Most organizations publish an employee manual, and it is often provided at this initial meeting. This is a prime opportunity for the human resources professional to interact positively with an employee.

But employers' needs for employees change over time. The marketplace may create new demands, products, and services. Outside economic conditions can create internal changes. Whatever the reason, most organizations are seldom static in terms of staffing needs, and the human resources professional is frequently asked to assess department needs for new personnel or to examine an area suspected of having an excess of workers. Consulting for this purpose, the human resources professional needs to understand the department and the various roles its workers play so he or she can effectively offer solutions to staffing issues. The result could be transfers of employees to other departments or even layoffs or termination. Because personnel costs often represent the largest consistent expense of an organization, the human resources' role here is critical to the financial success of an organization.

As a sociology major, you should have little difficulty in bringing your sociology studies to bear on the employment and placement activities of the organization. Issues of self-esteem, job definition and structure, and an employee's entry into a new organization are all significant issues. Your sensitivity to these issues will help you when working with department managers to define job parameters, when planning for interviewing procedures that give each candidate a fair chance, and when arranging to help a new employee make a successful transition into a new job.

Salary Administration

In many companies and nonprofit organizations, the largest percentage of the overall budget goes toward pay and benefits. As a result, human resources professionals dedicate a great deal of energy toward salary administration.

Basic salaries, opportunities for pay increases, and deductions for various benefits are of crucial importance to all employees. After all, pay is a basic need. Money guarantees the possibility of satisfying many of our needs, such as housing, food, and security. Understanding this, a sociology major will recognize how important it is to educate workers on their pay, on how it works, and the reasons for any changes in pay schedules.

A sociology major working in human resources will understand that many people define their work by their salary level, that people make comparisons to others of similar employment level, and that people are on the alert for any discrepancies or hints of discrimination. Wages, salaries, and related matters are sensitive and complex issues. The ramifications of these behaviors to the human resources department are significant. Many human resources departments regularly research the salaries paid by similar organizations for comparable jobs. In addition, if there are potential inconsistencies within your organization, those inconsistencies should be either eliminated or determined to be reasonable.

Employee Benefits Administration

When a new employee is hired, one of his or her first steps is meeting with human resources staff to fill out the forms for health insurance and other benefits. Providing the right benefits is critical, as is maintaining costs.

No human resources office is open for any length of time before the paperwork involved in the administration of benefits begins to accumulate. Requests for tuition reimbursement; workers' compensation; dental, medical, and optical care; pension planning; and 401(k)s pile up. The specific list varies from organization to organization as each offers a unique blend of employee benefits. Often, the benefits menu changes depending upon the status of the employee. Full-time employees receive a full complement of benefits, while those who work less than full time have their benefits prorated according to their percent-time worked or may receive no benefits. It adds up to a mountain of paperwork, both in "hard copy" and electronic form. Some employees tell horror stories of how human resources mismanaged one of their benefit claims, but far more will speak of excellent benefits and administrators who are sensitive and discreet in the processing of the ever-present forms.

At the same time, new benefits are always emerging. Some of the newer ones include spousal benefits for same-sex partnerships and supplemental health allowances for individuals requiring special diets and food supplements. Many firms are now dealing with the issues of drug and alcohol abuse among their workers and are developing programs that refer these employees for counseling and treatment to off-site employee assistant programs. Usually, these employees continue working or return to full employment following a course of treatment.

Most employers realize, moreover, that the physical and mental health of their employees plays a key role in productivity. When an organization provides exercise rooms or has a professional making mental health referrals, it knows it will see sharply reduced absenteeism, fewer claims on employee health and benefit programs, and increased productivity because of these efforts. So, while the human resources promotional literature emphasizes enhanced benefits to the employee, the real rewards are savings for the employer.

Benefits administration can be a deeply rewarding job for the sociology major, especially today, as organizations become ever more sensitive to human needs and the relationship between satisfying those needs and work productivity. You can hardly function well at work if you're worried about the hospitalization costs for your child's chronic illness. Sociology majors employed in human resources work will have many opportunities to review benefit options and consider new proposals that might directly answer employees' needs.

Training and Development
Keeping employees well trained and up to date in job knowledge is an important consideration. The training and development function in human resources provides continuing education opportunities for employees. This

training may be developed and delivered in-house by staff trainers, it may be purchased with a contract for a speaker or workshop facilitator, or it may involve sending employees off-site to attend educational conferences and symposia or to take college classes.

Depending on the number of employees and the size of the human resources department, training and development may be conducted in-house or contracted out to other professionals. Most organizations use a combination. In-house human resources professionals will offer workshops year-round on issues as diverse as retirement planning, safe driving, employee safety and health precautions, and using employee benefits effectively. Workshops on stress management and promotion opportunities may be provided along with new supervisor training programs. Outside professionals may be called in to do health screenings and education programs, as well as multicultural and diversity workshops.

You will find challenges and satisfaction in developing and delivering staff training programs. Workers value good on-the-job training and will often let you know it. Many issues are facing the workplace from accommodating those with disabilities to preventing or dealing with sexual harassment. Staff development not only builds a sense of employee cohesion and camaraderie, but it can also be a quick and deliberate response to critical issues facing the workplace and its employees. Some training programs are established and remain in place with modifications, only as needed, for years.

The sociology major looks out over the range and variety of employees in an organization and realizes that each person is at a different stage in his or her developmental life and career. Some are young and ambitious, eager for change and growth, and able to be flexible with their time and lives. Others are embarking on relationships or starting families and have chosen, for the present time, to concentrate their energies on those aspects of their lives. Some may be continuing their education, while others are anticipating slowing down their schedules, working less, and easing into retirement. Each individual is in a different place in work life, chronological age, and personal development as well as in commitment to the organization and the job, and your appreciation of these differences can spark ideas and strategies for wonderful and varied training and development programs.

The organization in general and the human resources worker in particular are primarily concerned with three types of development that create a cohesive workforce and achieve organizational missions and goals: (1) training and development, or developing key competencies in workers that enable them to carry out their duties; (2) organizational development, which primarily focuses on helping groups manage change; and (3) career development, which involves helping employees manage their careers within and beyond the organization.

Job Development. Most workers want to be proud of what they accomplish in their jobs, but they may need additional training to be able to work at their full potential. A computer data-entry worker may need to learn database management. A new supervisor may need to develop some conflict negotiation skills. In any of these kinds of situations, the human resources professional is responsible for ensuring that workers either come into the organization with the skills they need to do the assigned work or that mechanisms are available (courses, cross-training, self-tutoring programs) to allow the worker to develop those competencies.

Organizations today are very interested in the concept of cross-training—teaching workers to perform a variety of tasks. Workers learn each other's jobs, thus making their work more interesting and varied as well as allowing for greater flexibility in staffing and hiring.

Organizational Development. Organizations are undergoing stressful levels of change to maintain their strategic advantage in the marketplace. Whether the organization is a nonprofit that coordinates emergency relief efforts or a for-profit manufacturer producing the latest in computer chip technology, both require employees who can handle changing needs. The human resources department can help effect these changes through hiring procedures, employee training, and employee transitions within the organizations.

Many organizations are increasing their contacts outside of the United States and Canada. Foreign travel for management, including short-term and long-term job assignments, has become commonplace in many workplaces. The need for some bilingual employees, increased technology for overseas communication, and adjusting work hours to better coordinate with foreign markets are all competitive realities if an organization is to stay viable. Human resources helps to plan and implement these changes in a productive and nonthreatening manner.

Career Development. Job seekers face an ever-changing marketplace, one that demands flexibility to be able to handle organizational change. Human resources personnel may help employees take concrete and specific steps to manage their own careers within the organization, allowing each person to use a greater range of his or her skills and abilities to accomplish organizational goals.

Data Management. Record keeping and retrieval are critical in human resources work. That's why you'll see ads similar to this:

Records Management Manager. Growing manufacturing company needs bachelor's degree graduate in human resources management or a human service area for records management within human resources office. Strong computer skills and familiarity with current software packages required.

Requests for a history of workers' compensation claims, average salary increases for middle management, or any number of other employee topics frequently come in to the human resources department. Staff personnel need to be comfortable analyzing and providing data that will be useful to management in making staffing and other strategic decisions.

The Americans with Disabilities Act (ADA), Canadian Human Rights Act, contract negotiations and arbitration, the Equal Employment Opportunity initiatives, fair wages standards, and Occupational Safety and Health Administration (OSHA) guidelines as well as an organization's own internal grievance process all provide enormous amounts of paperwork.

Excellent record-keeping skills with an eye to data retrieval are required to meet these information needs. This is one of the many reasons why a human resources office is often very concerned with paperwork and administration. In fact, many entry-level employees are disappointed to discover their position involves as much paperwork (or more) as it does interactions with people.

As a sociology major, you should be able to handle the data required in the job, because you've not only had to complete numerous research reports in your studies, but you have probably created some data yourself, which you had to transform into meaningful information.

The Bottom-Line Role of the Human Resources Professional

A basic question for many human resources professionals is, "Do I serve the organization or the worker?" In the overwhelming majority of circumstances, the answer is that they serve the organization and seek to maintain the expectations of management. In areas such as job design, pay grades and classifications, promotion and job enhancement, training and development, benefits administration, and the arbitration of grievances and employee policies, human resources professionals are not advocates of employees but rather representatives of the employer, exercising that employer's mandates in the administration of the workforce.

On the other hand, human resources professionals can also serve as advocates for employees. Workers do grow in their jobs, often because of the policies and encouragement of human resources professionals. As a result, they may need to be reclassified to a higher rank. Human resources personnel design creative and innovative programs for workers that not only affect their work performance and relationships but can also influence other aspects of their lives. Human resources programs, depending on their size and breadth, can touch on life changes: parenthood, retirement, aging, and many other personal and family challenges.

None of this programming is done, however, without keeping in mind a strong sense of the organization's overall mission and the effect of these programs on the budget and use of human resources personnel. Human resources activities do not drive the organization; they support its principal mission and goals.

If you are seriously interested in pursuing this career path it is important to sit down and talk with a human resources professional about the negative or stressful aspects of the field. The human resources worker faces the anger of employees frustrated with benefits administration, changes in work conditions, salary negotiations, or promotion opportunities. You may be privileged to hear a human resources professional share what it's like to listen to the complaints and humiliation of a discharged employee who must be accompanied by a human resources official as he packs up his office and is escorted from the building. On occasion, there is the challenge of having to remove an employee with the help of security personnel. To have the full picture of this job, you need to hear both the positive and the negative.

The Right Qualifications

Many of the skills and attributes that will be important to a new human resources professional are suggested in the previous discussion. But others are important as well, including communication skills, presentation skills, computer literacy, and data analysis.

Communication Skills
In both oral and written communication, human resources professionals need to be very careful about the accuracy, tone, and nuance of their language.

Most of the issues dealt with in human resources departments are immensely important to employees, and work conditions can be vital to an employee's sense of self-esteem and identity. Change, even the suggestion of change, can provoke great anxiety among some employees. How such change is presented is crucial to the success of any plan. Strong—make that excellent—communication skills are required for maximum effectiveness.

For example, let's say your firm has decided to purchase a new telephone system that requires each employee to key in his or her own identification number for every call. Prior to this, phone charges have been anonymously lumped by department for each extension number. The unwritten policy has been that a reasonable number of personal phone calls (for example, calls home to your spouse) were OK. Now, with a new caller ID number, many employees will be concerned about the loss of that privilege. Realizing this is a concern, you may want to specifically address it in your memo and reassure employees that a reasonable number of personal calls is still acceptable.

One-on-one conferences, small group and department meetings, e-mails or memoranda, and policies and procedures manuals all need to contain clear and direct language that will enable all staff members to understand and carry out organizational policies. If time allows, you might, as a new human resources employee, take on the project of collecting and reviewing literature and human resources publications from other public organizations for sensitive and clear language. Analyzing the communication styles of these other publications should provide ideas for improving your own organizational communicating efforts.

Presentation Skills

The ability to speak before groups in an organized manner is another skill that may be needed in the human resources area.

Because many human resources programs affect many employees, it is often more efficient to present material to large groups. Professional staff need to have excellent public presentation skills, including the ability to plan, organize, and write a workshop or seminar; design and execute effective and appropriate visual materials; and design and execute forms for evaluation. Technical competency with audiovisual materials, including computer projectors and other state-of-the-art equipment and software, is certainly a plus.

If you've had experience with presentation hardware and software in college, be sure to feature that on your résumé or in a cover letter. Skilled presenters are always in demand, especially when they are comfortable with technology that can be used to improve retention and communication.

As with all administrative units, the use of computers in a human resources department is pervasive. Database management skills are crucial for data analysis and retrieval, as are word-processing skills that are used for employee communications. Many departments produce their own brochures and information pieces, and they rely on staff to create the newsletters to be distributed to employees.

Just as it is safe to assume that all human resources staff at every level employ some degree of computer use in this field, it is likewise a safe assumption that the entry-level candidate with strong computer skills stands a markedly increased opportunity for employment compared to the candidate who has neglected this technical competency.

Have you included your computer and data management courses on your résumé? If not, be sure to mention them in your cover letter or online application or during an interview. In reading about human resources, you've become aware of the vast amounts of data and detail that are going to be stored electronically. It's ironic, but true, that to perform your human resources task in a very human, connected manner with your employees, you need to be proficient with computer technology.

If you have a chance to talk with a human resources professional, ask about data technology and the expectations of the employer for computer skills. What should you have for an entry-level position and how much will you learn on the job? How much of the day's work is on the computer? Is there a human resources data analyst on the staff? Who inputs data? A discussion about computer technology will help you understand the importance of these skills in a human resources department.

Data Analysis

Data analysis allows the human resources professional to interpret and explain the meaning of the data. In effect, data analysis transforms otherwise meaningless data into useful information. To the hackneyed statement of many young job candidates for human resources positions that they're "a people person," most hiring professionals might chuckle and say most days they could use a good data analyst! The reality is, as with so many issues, somewhere in the middle of those two extremes lies the ideal candidate. An effective human resources department needs to provide management with good data analysis.

For every human interaction, be it a one-on-one meeting, a public presentation to a department or group of employees, or new staff orientation and briefing, a great deal of time is spent reading, analyzing, and discussing data concerning staff. Overtime and associated costs, sick days, temporary help expenditures, vacation scheduling and conflicts, and use of benefits all need to be monitored and understood.

You know from your course on methods of sociological research that data can reveal trends and indicate problems. You bring to your human resources job an ability to build a bridge from anonymous cold data to the real, live human interactions the data represents. Often, your time spent in reading the early warning signs in data can lead you right out of your office into the satisfying human interaction of conferences and meetings as you seek answers to questions and solutions to problems.

Earnings

How much you will earn as a human resources professional will depend on your place of employment and level of experience. According to the U.S. Department of Education, median annual earnings for human resources specialists in 2006 were as follows:

Compensation and benefits managers: $74,750
Training and development managers: $80,250
Other human resources managers: $88,510

For human resources managers employed by the U.S. federal government, the median income was $76,503 in 2007. Starting pay, naturally, is significantly lower. According to a 2007 salary survey conducted by the National Association of Colleges and Employers, bachelor's degree candidates majoring in human resources, including labor and industrial relations, received starting offers averaging $41,680 yearly. In Canada, average salaries range C$42,000 to C$72,000, according to Service Canada.

It's worth noting that even in a troubled economy, the base salaries in this field have a history of increasing faster than the national average for all occupations. Those employed in this field may earn incentive pay—often in the form of stock options—indicating the crucial role they play in the success of their organizations.

Career Outlook

The field of human resources is interesting in its diversity and scope. The number and types of positions in human resources vary dramatically, depending on the size of the organization, the state of its fiscal health, and the emphasis the organization puts on its employees and their welfare. Human resources is not a revenue-producing department. Unlike sales forces, for example, whose high working expenses (travel, meals, and accommodations) are offset by the generation of income for the firm, the human resources department is pure administration and is seen as overhead. Consequently, it is often earmarked during difficult economic times for trimming its staff or not filling empty positions to ensure greater profitability. The training and development division of many human resources departments is frequently the first target of such staff trimming.

Sociology majors looking for the most promising entry-level jobs in human resources would do best to select from among mid- to large-size organizations and the largest corporations. While many small, entrepreneurial firms enjoy profitability and growth, they seldom have the developed human resources function of the larger corporations.

Court rulings that affect the workplace, on issues such as occupational safety and health, equal employment opportunity, and family leave, will increase the demand for human resources workers. Moreover, companies hoping to avoid costly court cases will call on their own internal human resources departments to mediate labor-management disputes. And given the changing demographics of the United States and Canada, employees who have special skills in international human resources management will be needed.

Strategy for Finding the Jobs

One plus in this field is that human resources departments of whatever size are usually the easiest departments to locate in an organization! Most organizations, even the smallest, have someone designated to answer the telephone when the caller asks for personnel or human resources. And most organizations' websites have a prominent section for job seekers. Since locating human resources activity will not represent a challenge, your strategic efforts will focus more on how to handle each contact you make with a potential employer.

Human resources positions, especially entry-level ones, are filled by graduates who come from a variety of academic disciplines. You should expect that the level of competition for these positions will be keen. A job search in this field should revolve around the following suggestions. First, begin as early as you can in your college career to build a portfolio of expertise in human resources. Suggestions for doing so are discussed in the following sections. Second, you must be ready to explain to a potential employer how your sociology education has prepared you to work effectively in this field. Both your résumé and your interview comments must highlight the relevance of a sociology major to human resources. Finally, you will then need to identify employment settings that seem like a good fit for you to begin your human resources career.

Getting Relevant Experience

If possible, make sure to register for courses that are directly related to human resources. If there is a business school at your university, you might look into auditing courses in personnel or human/industrial relations or taking a minor in one of these areas. In addition, you should make an effort to obtain some hands-on experience in the field, perhaps in the form of a for-credit internship.

Don't neglect your own college or university human resources office, and inquire about internships there. Though there may be issues of confidentiality and discretion regarding student employees, generally these offices have numerous projects where you could make a contribution and learn more about the human resources function at the same time.

In addition to appropriate classes, be on the lookout for material focusing on current societal trends that affect the functions and mission of a human resources department as well as issues the human resources professional faces.

Stay Informed About Societal Trends. This chapter has provided a basic outline of this profession, but how it plays out in the field varies dramatically by organization, product, or service and even by geographic region. For example, many cutting-edge technological firms have instituted some of the newest—and often controversial—employee benefit programs. Many have proven comfortable with employees working from home part of the week, flextime, and loose organizational structures. Such policies might not succeed in a more traditional organization with a less sophisticated or less educated employment pool. A continued reading of business periodicals and the business section of newspapers will help you to become conversant with trends that affect the current state of human resources administration.

Learn the Legal Issues. Becoming more knowledgeable about the legal issues that increasingly dominate human resources management is an important part in preparing yourself for positions in this field. Some of the topics you'll want to be familiar with include the following:

- OSHA (Occupational Safety and Health Administration) or CCOHS (Canadian Centre for Occupational Health and Safety)
- Pension planning
- 401(k)s

- Medical claims/syndromes
- Ergonomics
- Arbitration
- Labor relations
- Negotiations
- Contracts
- Sexual harassment

You needn't become an expert on these topics, but they are important issues to human resources professionals. Your job search will be far more successful if you can demonstrate an awareness of and appreciation for these challenges. By doing so, you can overcome any hesitancy an employer may feel due to your lack of actual human resources experience. Your willingness to educate yourself is, in and of itself, a strong employment consideration.

Use your summer or part-time employment to find out as much as you can about working in human resources. If you cannot find employment in that area, working in an organization that has a professional human resources management department can be useful. You can network with the director or manager of human resources to let him or her know about your interests and to see if he or she can assist you in getting information or making contacts in the field. You may want to invest in a membership in a professional human resources organization (see the end of the chapter for suggestions) to further pursue your networking and to begin learning about actual employment opportunities.

Connecting the Dots

In seeking employment, you may need to help potential employers recognize the connection between sociology and human resources. Your sociology degree has helped you develop many skills that are important in working effectively in human resources. But those skills and that knowledge might not be readily apparent to potential employers. Don't let them guess about how well qualified you are. Show them on your résumé and in your interview. Point out your relevant training, and tell them how you can help accomplish their human resources goals.

Consider Yourself Your First Placement. The "Potential Employers" section of this path describes a wide range of employers. You may be able to picture yourself working in some settings, and you will know immediately that you wouldn't feel comfortable in others. Review the following section and make a decision about where you would like to begin your employment search. You may have to widen the scope, depending on the geographic area where you live and the types of employers you decide to focus on first. But start with an industry that looks like the best fit.

Potential Employers

Personnel, training, and labor relations specialists and managers are found in every industry, from manufacturing to banking and transportation to health care and education. Some of the possibilities include the following:

Education
Employment agencies
Finance and insurance
Government
Health care
Manufacturing
Service

Your job search should begin with a review of all types of possible employers. After you have familiarized yourself with the range of possibilities, begin your job search by starting to network with professionals, and then apply for jobs in one or more industries.

Education

Human resources is an important function in any educational institution. Elementary and secondary schools, community and two-year colleges, four-year colleges, and universities all hire a variety of workers to help them achieve their educational mission and goals. Whether it is the custodian who keeps the facility in shape, the teacher in the classroom, the support or technical staff member, or the administrator, all are important, and the human resources worker helps find the right person for the right job.

Help in Locating These Employers. To locate human resources jobs in education, check appropriate websites. For colleges or universities, simply access their websites and look under "jobs" or "employment." For public schools, check at the district level rather than with individual schools. Also be sure to consult publications such as the *Chronicle of Higher Education*, which features extensive job listings.

Temp Firms and Employment Agencies

The role of employment agencies in the workplace, providing either temporary or permanent hires, has grown dramatically. Rather than hiring a regular employee, many organizations will instead hire a field staffer (temporary employee) to try out. If all goes well, the staffer may be offered regular employment. In some large organizations, however, the situation creates a schism in the workforce. Often, temporary workers do not receive the same benefits that accrue to regular salaried employees, even though these temporary workers might be working long-term assignments at a given organization. At the same time, the hourly wages for temporary workers—not counting the benefits such as health insurance—are sometimes higher than for those filling similar roles at the same company.

The agencies that fill these temporary postings need professionals, including graduates with sociology degrees, on their own staffs. Sociology graduates might start out as service coordinators and be responsible for interviewing and orienting applicants, testing them, and making a decision as to whether the agency wants to work with them. They evaluate job orders, locate and refer qualified applicants, and write job advertisements. In this industry, service coordinators can move into positions in sales, marketing, and management once they have paid their dues as service coordinators.

Help in Locating These Employers. One easy way to begin locating employment agencies is to review the yellow pages for the geographic area where you would like to work. Yellow pages directories are available in many larger public and college libraries. Your local phone company business office may also be able to provide you with some directories for a fee. Look under Employment Agencies, Employment Contractors—Temporary Help, and Employment Service—Employee Leasing. You will probably be surprised at the number of agencies listed.

Web searches can be similarly helpful. Just use search terms such as "temporary services," "temp jobs," or "employment agencies," and add a geographical descriptor to narrow your search.

Insurance and Finance

The financial services sector includes commercial banks, savings institutions, credit unions, mutual fund companies, securities firms, venture capital firms, commodities futures trading companies, and insurance companies. Telecommunications capabilities have significantly changed the way this industry does its work, and some sociology majors will be particularly interested in the effect of this new technology on the workforce. The human resources department in industries with cutting-edge technology will play a valuable role in maintaining worker cohesiveness and job satisfaction.

Help in Locating These Employers. If you would like to begin generating a list of possible employers, begin by accessing career websites such as the following:

CareerBuilder.com (careerbuilder.com)
Canadajobs.com (canadajobs.com)
Current Jobs for Graduates (graduatejobs.com)
JobHunt (job-hunt.org)
Monster (monster.com)

Also check out websites of major insurance companies, banks, or other financial institutions.

Your career office can also provide you with corporate literature on finance and insurance organizations that have recruited at the college or university level. And don't forget to check the yellow pages for organizations in business in your area. Other sources of job informantion include professional associations and the classified sections of newspapers (both print and online versions).

Federal Agencies

Chapter 8 contains up-to-date information on both the federal hiring process and those departments and agencies most interested in sociology graduates. Because of the nature of the federal job classification system, sociology graduates are considered to be qualified applicants for entry-level human resources generalist positions in the federal workforce. The federal government is the largest employer in the United States and, in times of uncertainty, is a source of secure jobs with predictable rates of promotion. The sociology major working in human resources can help screen, process, and train the best candidates for federal government positions and administer operations relating to personnel functions.

In some ways, the hiring process has become simpler. Online government job sources, such as USAJOBS (usajobs.gov), list thousands of federal openings throughout the United States as well as international positions. You may also contact the Office of Personnel Management (OPM) directly and speak with a personnel assistant. OPM has regional offices that are responsible for their area's human resources, and you can begin by applying for work at those offices. In addition, you may now contact and apply directly to individual agencies and departments online.

In Canada, the best place to start is the Public Service Commission (PSC) of Canada, which manages a process not unlike that followed in the United States. To find job openings and related information, access its website at jobs.gc.ca.

Help in Locating These Employers. A great place to get started in learning more about options in government employment is the *Occupational Outlook Handbook*, published by the U.S. Department of Labor. Along with a wealth of career profiles in virtually every employment area, this publication profiles job categories in the federal government, opportunities for liberal arts majors, and tips to assist aspiring federal employees. The *OOH* contains information on federal pay scales and tips on how to apply to agencies and application process alternatives. Addresses for the human resources functions of the largest executive departments and excepted agencies are given. Contact those you may be interested in working for to determine their hiring procedures.

In addition, resources such as *Government Jobs in America*, *Government Job Finder*, and *Careers in Nonprofits and Government Agencies* can be helpful.

State, Provincial, and Local Government Agencies

State, provincial, and larger local governments offer human resources positions that help in staffing departments that include corrections, court systems, education, fire protection, health, highway and street construction, housing and community development, hospitals, libraries, natural resources, parks and recreation, police, sanitation, transportation, utilities, and welfare services. Your background in sociology has helped prepare you to process, test, and screen applicants who will be interviewed by the various departments.

Help in Locating These Employers. Begin your search by checking with the personnel or human resources office for the state, provincial, or local governmental agency you would like to work for. These offices can tell you how they advertise for open positions, and they can provide application forms that may be required or refer you to online application materials. An especially helpful resource is the section of USAJOBS dedicated to state and local employment opportunities (thejobpage.gov/statelocal.asp). Another useful site is GovJobs (govjobs.com). In Canada, a similar resource is

The Work Place; go to theworkplace.ca and click on the "government" heading.

Health Care
The dramatically changing face of health care in the United States will continue to provide opportunities for human resources professionals. Health care delivery facilities employ doctors, nurses, technicians, food-service workers, maintenance workers, administrators, managed-care coordinators, social workers, and a host of other types of employees. The human resources professional can play a critical role in filling positions with the right people.

Help in Locating These Employers. You should review several resources as you conduct your job search, including the American Hospital Association's *AHA Guide to U.S. Hospitals, Health Care Systems, Networks, Alliances, Health Organizations, Agencies & Providers.* Also take advantage of all the info available at Pam Pohly's Net Guide at www.pohly.com. Be sure to directly contact those health organizations you would like to work for, and do some informational interviewing or inquire about their procedures for advertising job openings.

Manufacturing
Whether a company is manufacturing cell phones, hats and gloves, computer microchips, or trucks and automobiles, human resources personnel have screened, processed, oriented, trained, and/or provided benefits to the labor force. As the United States and Canada fight to maintain their competitiveness in manufacturing, it needs competent human resources workers to assemble a well-qualified group of employees.

Help in Locating These Employers. A solid resource to start with is Hoover's (hoovers.com), which provides thousands of company overviews. Business.com (business.com) is another helpful site. You may want to become familiar with the Standard Industrial Coding (SIC) scheme, which groups manufacturers producing similar products, to find environments in which you are interested in working. Contact your local Chamber of Commerce for assistance in identifying manufacturing firms operating in your area.

Service
No matter where you go, whether in food retailing, household furniture and appliance sales, clothing sales, travel services, or business and professional services, personnel are available to assist you. Medium- to large-sized organiza-

tions have human resources professionals who help them hire people willing to work to support organizational goals and serve customers.

Help in Locating These Employers. Because the service industry is so large, be sure to ask the other professionals you are working with, such as career counselors and librarians, for recommendations. The business reference section of your college library will also have a number of directories that you can review. Hoover's (hoovers.com) and Business.com (business.com) are just as helpful for service industries as they are with manufacturing firms. Another resource is ThomasNet (thomasnet.com); see this site's "services" heading for relevant information.

Possible Job Titles

Because human resources workers can be generalists or specialists, depending on the size and complexity of the organization, you will see quite a range of job titles. Consider them all to decide which positions you're qualified to fill or to determine an area that you would like to specialize in.

Affirmative action coordinator
Arbitrator
Benefits administrator
Benefits analyst
Benefits manager
Compensation manager
Compensation specialist
Education specialist
Employee assistance plan manager
Employee benefits manager
Employee development specialist
Employee relations representative
Employee welfare office/manager
Employer relations representative
Employment interviewer
Employment specialist
Equal Employment Opportunity (EEO) representative
Grievance officer

Human resources coordinator
Human resources information systems specialist
Human resources manager
Human resources specialist
Industrial relations manager/director
Industrial relations specialist
International human resources manager
Interviewer
Job analyst
Job classification specialist
Labor relations specialist
Management analyst
Mediator
Occupational analyst
Personnel administrator
Personnel consultant
Personnel director
Personnel management specialist
Personnel officer
Personnel staffing specialist
Position classification specialist
Position classifier
Position review specialist
Recreation specialist
Recruiter
Salary administrator
Service coordinator
Test development specialist
Trainer
Training and development manager
Training specialist

Professional Associations

Several associations serve those interested in pursuing a career in human resources. Review the listings shown below and decide whether any of the groups can provide information relevant to your job search.

American Arbitration Association (AAA)
1633 Broadway, 10th Floor
New York, NY 10019
adr.org
Members/Purpose: Businesses, unions, trade and educational associations, law firms, arbitrators, and other interested individuals.
Publications: *Dispute Resolution Journal, Arbitration and the Law, AAA Handbook on Mediation*, other handbooks
Training: Offers online workshops, seminars, conferences, and skill-building sessions
Job Listings: Regional offices sometimes have listings; contact AAA for regional office nearest you

American Society for Healthcare Human Resources Administrators (ASHHRA)
c/o American Hospital Association
One North Franklin
Chicago, IL 60606
hrleader.org
Members/Purpose: To provide effective and continuous leadership in the field of health care human resources administration.
Publications: *Leaders Voice*, case studies
Job Listings: Offers placement service

American Society for Training and Development (ASTD)
1640 King Street, Box 1443
Alexandria, VA 22313-2043
astd.org
Members/Purpose: Professional association for persons from more than 100 companies engaged in the training and development of business, industry, education, and government.
Publications: *T&D* magazine, *T&D* webcasts, *The Buzz, ASTD Links, execuBooks*
Training: Sponsors meetings; maintains database of seminars, workshops, and conferences, and training materials from various suppliers
Job Listings: Offers online Job Bank

American Staffing Association (ASA)
277 South Washington Street, Suite 200
Alexandria, VA 22314
americanstaffing.net

Members/Purpose: Companies supplying workers to other firms on a temporary basis.
Publications: *Staffing Week* newsletter, *Staffing Success* magazine, *Staffing Law*
Training: Offers certification program
Job Listings: Offers tips and information for job seekers

Canadian Council of Human Resources Associations (CCHRA)
150 Metcalfe Street, Suite 603
Ottawa, ON K2P 1P1
cchra-ccarh.ca
Members/Purpose: Represents more than 33,000 professionals, including over 16,000 Certified Human Resources Professionals (CHRPs). Fosters enhancement and promotion of the human resources profession across Canada. Collaborates on national issues related to the profession; influences federal government relations and international human resources issues.
Publications: *National CHRP Registry*
Training: Sponsors national HR forums; offers a national certification process
Job Listings: None

College and University Personnel Association for Human Resources
1811 Common Points Drive
Knoxville, TN 37932
cupahr.org
Members/Purpose: Professional organization made up of colleges and universities interested in the improvement of campus human resources administration.
Publications: *CUPA-HR Journal, CUPA-HR eNews*
Training: Sponsors national and regional conferences, webinars, web-based Knowledge Center
Job Listings: Offers online JobLine with openings searchable by keyword and by region

International Association of Workforce Professionals (IAWP)
1801 Louisville Road
Frankfort, KY 40601
iawponline.org
Members/Purpose: Officials and others engaged in job placement and unemployment-compensation administration through municipal, state,

provincial, and federal government employment agencies and unemployment compensation agencies.

Publications: *Workforce Professional, Chapter Activity Countdown, IAWP Handbook for Administration*

Training: Conducts workshops and offers professional development programs at the district, chapter, and subchapter levels, as well as a Certified Workforce Specialist Program

Job Listings: None

International Foundation of Employee Benefit Plans
Box 69
18700 West Bluemound Road
Brookfield, WI 53045
ifebp.org

Members/Purpose: Jointly trusteed, public, Canadian, and company-sponsored employee benefit plans. Administrators, labor organizations, employer associations, benefit consultants, investment counselors, insurance consultants, banks, attorneys, accountants, actuaries, and others who service or are interested in the field of employee benefit plans.

Publications: *Benefits & Compensation Digest, Canadian Benefits and Compensation Digest, Public Employee Quarterly, Small Business Quarterly*

Training: Cosponsors the Certified Employee Benefit Specialist Program, a ten-course college-level study program leading to a professional designation in the employee benefits field

Job Listings: Provides online job listings; allows members to post résumés online

International Public Management Association for Human Resources
1617 Duke Street
Alexandria, VA 22314
ipma-hr.org

Members/Purpose: Public human resources agencies and individuals (personnel workers, consultants, teachers); seeks to improve human resources practices in government.

Publications: *HR News, Public Personnel Management, HR Bulletin,* membership directory

Training: Sponsors seminars and workshops on public human resources administration

Job Listings: Offers online job postings

National Association of Personnel Services (NAPS)
131 Prominence Court
Dawsonville, GA 30534
recruitinglife.com
Members/Purpose: Private employment agencies.
Publications: Membership directory, certification manuals, brochures
Training: Conducts certification program; holds annual conferences and other meetings
Job Listings: None

National Association of State Personnel Executives (NASPE)
c/o Council of State Governments
2760 Research Park Drive
P.O. Box 11910
Lexington, KY 40578
naspe.net
Members/Purpose: Personnel directors for state and territorial governments.
Publications: *NASPE E-xcutive, Inside NASPE*
Job Listings: Offers link to Jobs in Government website

Society for Human Resource Management (SHRM)
1800 Duke Street
Alexandria, VA 22314
shrm.org
Members/Purpose: Professional organization of human resources, personnel, and industrial relations executives.
Publication: *HR Magazine*
Training: Sponsors meetings; offers certification program and other resources
Job Listings: Operates online job site

WorldatWork (formerly American Compensation Association)
14040 North Northsight Boulevard
Scottsdale, AZ 85260
worldatwork.org
Members/Purpose: Managerial and professional-level administrative personnel in business, industry, and government responsible for the

establishment, execution, administration, or application of compensation practices and policies in their organization.

Publications: *WorldatWork Journal,* workspan magazine, workspan newsletter, *CanadianNews* e-newsletter

Training: Organizes numerous courses and seminars; offers certification program

Job Listings: Offers online Job Center

8

Path 4:
Public Employment

The connections between sociology, government, and the nonprofit sector are many. In fact, as a sociology major, you no doubt have read numerous studies that tie in to the realm of public policy and government services. At the federal, state, provincial, and local levels, sociologists are engaged in researching social trends, compiling data, facilitating government services, and helping form government policies. The materials compiled by government agencies are critical to the ongoing work of sociologists in academia as well as in other fields. You've certainly seen federal studies cited in your readings numerous times. Moreover, the federal government is the largest supplier of funding for many social service endeavors and is the architect of countless national programs, including welfare, unemployment, aid to families with dependent children, and other social service organizations. In recent years, state, provincial, and local governments have increasingly taken on projects and funding for initiatives once shouldered by the federal government. As a result, the bureaucracy for human service workers and social service departments on the state, provincial, and local levels has escalated dramatically.

The World of Public Careers

With the integral connection between government and the realm of sociology, it won't surprise you to find a chapter on this career path. Although you might have expected it, you may still be thinking that a government job is not for you. After all, you've probably read the bad press that governmental agencies often receive, and perhaps you don't want to be part of that.

As a sociology student, however, you know enough not to believe everything you hear or read online or in the papers. Too many generalizations are propagated about governmental agencies. Your education has taught you to look beyond the superficial and discover what's really going on. In this chapter, that's what we'll do. We'll examine the opportunities that exist in every aspect of government and discover exactly what kinds of jobs and work are available. You'll raise your public employment IQ and learn that not only does government present attractive opportunities to the sociology major, but that working for a governmental agency at the federal, state, provincial, or local level may also prolong and enhance your career.

Consider the concept of bureaucracy, for example. Your negative image may include concepts such as regimentation, boredom, routine tasks, and lack of advancement. Nothing could be farther from the truth. In fact, it is the overwhelming size of the government bureaucracy that has dictated the need for a correspondingly large bureaucratic structure. This is not, in and of itself, a bad thing. The public sector has led the way in introducing many innovative work concepts. This includes cross-training of employees to increase job satisfaction, job sharing for more flexible time schedules, and standardization of qualifications for promotion that have opened senior ranks to all qualified candidates regardless of gender, race, sexual orientation, or religion. Sadly, many private organizations remain much more rigid in job categorization and are often accused of politics and prejudice in the workplace. Public sector work units are often far smaller than many private organizations and no different than any workplace in appearance, energy, and professionalism.

Portable Skills

Developing portable skills—ones that you can take with you from job to job—is a recurrent theme in the Great Jobs series. These sorts of skills don't depend on a particular job vocabulary or knowledge of some economic sector. Nor are they relegated to certain geographic areas. They are job talents that you can apply in varying degrees to any job. Portable skills give you the flexibility to take on new jobs and challenges and qualify you to consider a wider range of employment.

Today's job market remains volatile. Downsizing and reductions in staffing continue to shift workers in and out of the job market. If you stay aware of trends in the workforce and develop those work skills that you can transfer from one job to another, you can look forward to a lengthy and productive work life. Public sector jobs provide excellent access to technology, the opportunity to enhance your computer expertise (a portable skill), and a heavy emphasis on training and professional development. Most important, these jobs require you to interact with a number of other public sector institutions as well as nonprofit organizations, trade and professional groups, law firms, contracting and consulting firms, research organizations, and international organizations and groups.

It is impossible to do justice to all your public sector employment possibilities in just one chapter. So, consider these pages the first chapter in your own book on public sector employment possibilities. As you'll see, a great deal of information is available directly from the government itself, which has set up websites to answer questions from those seeking a career in the public sector. In addition, resources such as *The Book of U.S. Government Jobs* (Bookhaven Press, 2008) and *Government Jobs in America* (Government Job News, 2008) provide useful information.

Working for the Federal Government

If someone asks you, "Who hires sociology majors?" the federal government should be your first response. It will also be the best answer to that question. The U.S. government has always been respectful and appreciative of the potential of liberal arts graduates, especially in the social sciences. The federal government is the largest single employer in the country. More than 1.9 million people work for the U.S. federal government in more than one hundred government agencies, boards, bureaus, commissions, and departments. Many of these governmental units are directly focused on the social life, changes, and causes of human behavior. Certain jobs require a general four-year degree, while others emphasize a particular major. A graduate or professional degree is necessary for some professional jobs.

Some of the departments hiring the largest number of college graduates (regardless of major) include the departments of Veterans Affairs, Defense, Agriculture, Interior, Commerce, Transportation, Education, the Treasury, and Energy, as well as Housing and Urban Development and the Environmental Protection Agency. College graduates may also find work in special government agencies, such as the Peace Corps and the National Institutes of Health. There are more white-collar, professional, and administrative positions in the federal government than there are in the economy overall. These jobs are also often much more relevant to your sociology degree.

Demand for Social Scientists

Another consideration in seeking public employment is the nature of government agency work and the qualifications the agencies desire in candidates for that work. Governments seek a greater number of employees who have an educational background in the social sciences than do nongovernmental agencies. It can be a bit of a challenge to determine exactly what specific qualifications the government is seeking. Luckily, the federal government's own websites and informational brochures can provide some of the answers.

For example, one government resource prepared by the Office of Personnel Management (OPM) listed the federal jobs that are often filled by college graduates with appropriate college majors. The list is not exhaustive, and a sociology major can find many additional opportunities. And some fields that might particularly appeal to sociology majors in fact call for the background provided by just about any major in college. These include the following:

- Administrative officer
- Civil rights analyst
- Contact representative
- Environmental protection specialist
- General investigator
- Logistics manager
- Management analyst
- Paralegal specialist
- Personnel administrator
- Public affairs officer
- Writer and editor

There are also career paths in the government that specifically call for sociology majors.

- General Accounting Office (GAO) evaluator
- Program analyst
- Social science aide and technician
- Social scientist
- Social service aide and assistant
- Social service representative
- Sociologist

Pursuing a Federal Job

Some people claim that you need to major in "Getting a Federal Job" to seek a position in the federal government. While getting a job in government can be a complex process, however, there is no "gatekeeper" trying to keep you out of the system. Indeed, the federal government has taken extraordinary steps to use the Internet to inform people about how to find the right federal job and has even made it possible to do all of your job searching as well as applying online. It still can be a disconcerting process, but when one remembers that the government is the largest employer in the country, it must not be impossible! Simply put, the federal application and screening process requires skill and care. That certainly may help to weed out those who are easily discouraged, have difficulty doing research, or find forms and documents an impossible challenge. The federal employment process probably does play a small part in self-selecting good candidates. All you have to learn is enough to make the system work for you.

Federal workers are classified into two major groups. First are those paid according to the General Schedule (GS), largely the white-collar, professional, administrative, scientific, clerical, and technical employees. This is the category offering employment that most college graduates will find attractive. The other classification is trade and labor, which employs those who support the efforts of the armed forces. These individuals are paid under the Federal Wage System (WG).

Salaries in governmental jobs, except in some specific areas, tend to be higher than competitive private sector jobs. This makes the government attractive as an employer, increases its pool of candidates, and allows it to skim the cream off the top, selecting the best and most qualified. A recently published General Schedule (GS) pay scale is included later in this chapter. Entry-level positions for most college graduates begin at the GS-5 or GS-7 level.

The Application Process

The federal application process has become somewhat easier in recent years, largely because of developments in the online exchange of information. While the federal government still demands more information than many private sector employers concerning your education, work experience, and personal background, the informational demands have been scaled down, and in many cases, personal questions are not posed until you are a finalist for the position.

One of the most exciting developments is that the Office of Personnel Management has made it possible to apply for federal jobs online. The USAJOBS site, at usajobs.gov, contains very detailed information on federal jobs, including listings and step-by-step descriptions of the process.

For Canadian citizens, the Public Service Commission (PSC) of Canada manages a process similar to that followed in the United States. For information on job openings, check out jobs.gc.ca. Here you'll find job profiles, job postings (including opportunities for both students and graduates), job search tools, an overview about working for government agencies, and more.

Following is a description provided by the U.S government's OPM of the hiring process followed by government agencies.

How Federal Jobs Are Filled. Many federal agencies fill their jobs like private industry by allowing applicants to contact the agency directly for job information and application processing. Most federal agencies are responsible for their own hiring actions. Résumés are preferred when applying; however, the Optional Application for Federal Employment, OF 612, is also accepted. Also, most positions do not require a written test. While the process is similar to that in private industry, there are differences due to the laws, executive orders, and regulations that govern federal employment.

Competitive and Excerpted Service. There are two classes of jobs in the federal government:

1. Those in the competitive civil service, and
2. Those in the excepted service.

Competitive service jobs are subject to the civil service laws passed by Congress to ensure that applicants and employees receive fair and equal treatment in the hiring process. A basic principle of federal employment is that all candidates must meet the qualification requirements before they are hired into the position.

Excepted service agencies set their own qualification requirements and are not subject to the same Congressional laws; however, they are subject to Veterans' preference. Some federal agencies, such as the Federal Bureau of Investigations (FBI) and the Central Intelligence Agency (CIA), have only excepted service positions. Other agencies may have both types of positions.

Announcing Positions. Agencies are required to post their competitive service positions on OPM's USAJOBS system whenever they are seeking applicants from the general public and outside of their own agency. Although agencies are not required to post their excepted service positions on USAJOBS, many do so they can get additional applicants. Remember, an agency is under no obligation to make a selection. In some instances, an agency may cancel the posting and choose to reannounce the vacancy at a later time.

USAJOBS is the federal government's official employment information system. On USAJOBS, you can explore more than fifteen thousand jobs on any given day, build and store up to five résumés for applying to federal jobs, and access a wide range of information about federal agencies and different federal employment issues. USAJOBS is also accessible by telephone at (703) 724-1850 or TDD (978) 461-8404. The USAJOBS phone system affords job seekers the same access to job and employment information as the website.

Applying for Positions. Most federal agencies do their own recruiting and hiring. Agencies post their announcements on USAJOBS with all the instructions and procedures for applying for that particular position. Because agencies do their own hiring and have different requirements, procedures and information required often vary among agencies. All agencies require the basic résumé information, but the amount of additional information needed for the agency to process your application varies. Examples include transcripts, forms, narrative descriptions of competencies, questionnaires, and so on. Follow the instructions very carefully, because information not submitted can result in your application not being evaluated.

Many announcements allow applicants to apply online directly to the agency. Using the online method, you decide which résumé to submit for that particular job. Contact information at the agency is also given in the announcement. If you have questions, call or e-mail the contact person.

To get started in filing an online application for employment, you'll be asked to create a personal profile. This process will help you avoid repeating the same steps every time you apply to a position. After completing your personal profile, you can continue with the online submission of your application.

The federal government and civil service jobs in general can provide solid employment prospects, but competition is keen. You will need to ensure that your résumé document is competitively professional, error-free, and as explicit about your experience and qualifications as you can make it. Government jobs can provide excellent, highly competitive incomes, superior working conditions, and, to many who are employed in this sector, an ambiance and atmosphere no different from any other sophisticated major employer. Your effort in the application process, however challenging, is well worth it.

For additional information about federal employment issues, visit the frequently asked questions section of USAJOBS at usajobs.opm.gov. You can also access that site from the websites of individual agencies and departments.

Federal Departments and Agencies

As noted previously, a number of governmental agencies routinely hire large numbers of college graduates. Some of the larger federal agencies and departments that hire workers with an educational background specifically in sociology include the Department of Agriculture, the Department of Health and Human Services, the Drug Enforcement Administration (Justice), the Environmental Protection Agency, Immigration and Customs Enforcement (Department of Homeland Security), and the United States Information Agency. Federal mailing addresses and telephone numbers for personnel offices change frequently, so the most reliable way to find the current contact numbers is to go to the agencies' websites, which are updated frequently.

Department of Agriculture (USDA). This department and its divisions work to improve farm income, to expand overseas markets for farm products, and to assure consumers of an adequate food supply at reasonable prices. The department works to safeguard the wholesomeness of our food supply through inspection of processing plants and ensures food quality through voluntary food-grading services. The USDA provides nutrition education and food assistance programs. The Department of Agriculture is a highly decentralized organization with a permanent workforce of approximately ninety-two thousand employees in all states of the union and several foreign countries. It recruits graduates with bachelor's degrees in sociology for positions in personnel management and as management analysts.

For more information, go to usda.gov.

Drug Enforcement Administration (DEA). The DEA in the Department of Justice is the principal federal law enforcement agency involved in combating drug abuse. The agency hires both bachelor's and master's degree holders in sociology to work as intelligence research specialists at the GS-5, 7, and 9 levels. (GS-5 and GS-7 are pay levels generally reserved for recent college graduates with or without experience. GS-9 is most often used to recognize either an advanced degree and/or significant work history in the field.) The DEA was established to control narcotics and drug abuse more effectively through enforcement and prevention. In carrying out its mission, the DEA cooperates with other federal agencies and with foreign as well as state and local governments, private industry, and other organizations. Its objectives are to reach all levels of the source of supply and to seize the greatest possible quantity of illegal drugs before they reach the user. To achieve its mission, the DEA has stationed highly trained agents along the numerous routes of illicit traffic, both in the United States and in foreign countries.

For more information, go to dea.gov.

Environmental Protection Agency (EPA). Approximately eighteen thousand people work for the EPA in numerous locations throughout the country. Sociology majors at both the undergraduate- and graduate-degree level are sought by the EPA for positions as environmental protection specialists. The mission of the EPA is to protect the health and welfare of the American people by preventing and cleaning up pollution hazards. The EPA endeavors to:

- Restore America's waters
- Reduce air pollution
- Clean up hazardous waste sites
- Formulate a comprehensive approach to other environmental problems, including the manufacture, use, and disposal of chemicals (pesticides and other potentially hazardous substances), radiation, and solid waste

The agency tries to accomplish its mission systematically by integrating its various activities of research, monitoring, standard setting, and enforcement. Overall, the EPA strives to formulate and implement policies that lead to a compatible balance between the often deleterious effects of human activities and the efforts of natural systems to support and nurture life.

To apply for a job at the EPA, use the USAJOBS website. You can also learn more at the agency's webpages on careers at epa.gov/careers. For more information about the agency itself, go to epa.gov.

Immigration and Customs Enforcement. More than forty-one thousand employees make up the Department of Homeland Security's U.S. Immigration and Customs Enforcement (ICE). This agency hires sociology majors at the bachelor's and master's degree level for a large number of occupations, with many employees working in one of the three hundred ports of entry along our land and sea borders.

Immigration and Customs Enforcement plays a major role in the nation's security. Along with working to stop drug trafficking and money laundering, ICE protects the public as well as labor and business by enforcing trademark, copyright, and patent privileges. Modern computer technology and communications are used extensively to facilitate the processing and security screening of the millions of passengers entering the United States by air, land, or sea each year. Merchandise processing is being streamlined through the use of sophisticated automation, and science and analytical research assist customs officers in their efforts to stop illegal and fraudulent activities. Increasing emphasis is being placed on the investigation of schemes that defraud the U.S. government of rightful revenue, on the illicit transportation of currency, and on export violations including the illegal shipment of arms and technology abroad.

For more information, go to ice.gov.

Department of Homeland Security. The Office of Homeland Security was established following the terrorist attacks of 2001 to develop and coordinate a comprehensive national strategy to protect the United States from terrorist threats and attacks. The office works with federal, state, and local governments, collecting information and ensuring that national preparedness programs and activities are developed and regularly evaluated.

Along with its work in coordinating the efforts of other government agencies, the department has stepped up efforts to recruit individuals for positions in all aspects of homeland readiness and security. These include positions with the U.S. Immigration and Customs Enforcement, the U.S. Capitol Police, the U.S. Coast Guard, the Federal Bureau of Investigation (FBI), the Federal Emergency Management Agency (FEMA), the Food and Drug Administration (FDA), and the Transportation Security Administration. Other agencies have also increased their staffs to meet the new standards of security.

For more information about positions supporting homeland readiness and security, go to usajobs.opm.gov. For more information about the Department of Homeland Security, go to dhsi.gov.

Definition of the Career Path

Your advancement as a sociologist within your federal position will be a function of your time in the position and any advanced education you may undertake. For example, candidates for the GS-7 and above rank must have either professional experience or graduate education (or a combination of both) in addition to the basic requirements (undergraduate degree in sociology with some course work in sociological research methods). This professional experience or graduate work must be directly related to sociology.

In addition to the basic requirements, the following professional experience is required for grades GS-7 and above:

Grade	Minimum Professional Experience (years)
GS-7	1
GS-9	2
GS-11 & above	3

In addition to the experience and the basic requirements, the following educational requirements exist for grades GS-7 and above:

Grade	Minimum Educational Requirements
GS-7	One full academic year of graduate education
GS-9	Master's or equivalent degree or two full years of graduate education
GS-11	Doctoral degree (Ph.D. or equivalent) or three full years of graduate education

Entry-level career opportunities in the federal government are widely advertised, and detailed job specifications are available for all but the most classified occupations. Although the application process may initially appear to be challenging, the screening and interviewing processes are fair and impartial, and diversity is welcomed and encouraged. Entry-level positions are classified according to government pay grades and promotions, and advancement opportunities are clearly indicated. Unlike many civilian occupations, the career path in most governmental jobs can be well defined. During your interview process, you should be prepared to discuss career-path possibilities with representatives of the agency or department you are applying to.

The Working Environment

It's truly impossible to make any generalizations about where people work in the federal government. Any working situation in the private sector can be found in duplicate in the public sector, and indeed there are thousands of federal employees on loan to private sector employers as consultants. Federal employees work in offices, hospitals, laboratories, aircraft hangars, warehouses, shipyards, construction sites, or outdoors in national parks or forests, even on Arctic research stations! Some work in very structured environments, others in very relaxed work settings, while still others may be involved in hazardous or stressful conditions.

It is difficult and not particularly responsible to try to make generalizations about the largest employer in the United States. The application process, even learning about job openings, is an indication of the size and complexity of the employer. But once hired, is it so different from any other job? Yes and no. The federal government shares many of the advantages and disadvantages of a very, very large employer. There is bureaucracy, red tape, some forced mobility, and some loss of personalization. There are also excellent salaries, benefits, career advancement, and training opportunities. Mobility may be an attraction for some. Many minorities have declared that the federal government offers them the most level playing field for success. The advantages of the federal system may be seen by some as disadvantages—the regularity and stability of government employment, for instance.

Many a federal employee will tell you that the working conditions of his or her job are no different from the private sector. Alternative work schedules, including flextime and compressed work schedules, are available to many. Some government agencies are even experimenting with flexible schedules and telecommuting to allow workers to work at home. Many larger federal sites have on-site day care for working parents. Most government jobs make fewer out-of-hours demands on their staff than private sector jobs do. Most federal agencies have some type of Quality of Work Life or Employee Involvement program that encourages employee participation at all levels for the purposes of improving efficiency, productivity, and working conditions. Some issues of working conditions that surface in any conversation on federal employment include job security, bureaucracy, politics, and public opinion.

Job Security. Government jobs become more appealing during times of economic instability. They provide stability, as well as a sense of purpose. While the salaries in public sector work are often lower than those in the private sector, the predictable schedule of promotions and raises, as well as the excellent benefits, make government jobs a logical choice for many. While there has been some elimination of government departments over time, the more recent picture is one of security and growth. Indeed, the Office of Personnel Management estimates that more than 50 percent of federal employees at the supervisory level will become eligible for retirement in the next six years.

The stability and regularity of government salaries are seen by some as an advantage and by others as a distinct disadvantage. If the economy does well or if an individual employee excels dramatically in his or her job, the private sector can respond with increases in salary. This is not possible in a federal job.

Bureaucracy. Federal employment will take a long time to live down complaints of bureaucracy. The truth is, just as the federal government has streamlined and dramatically simplified its employment practices, it is paying equal attention to unnecessary paperwork, rules, and constraints in every other aspect of its business. Innovation, minimizing red tape, and risk taking are equally valued by the federal sector and private employers.

Politics. Without a doubt, the overall shape and drive of government is responsive to the political party in office. This response, however, is rather diffuse and slow. New administrations can bring about large-scale changes in government management, but many day-to-day decisions are not affected by political considerations. Federal employees are no more political than any other group of employees, though unlike their private sector counterparts, they may pay more attention to news of the political process.

Public Opinion. In general, the public has not had a very positive image of federal employees and the jobs they do. One reason lies in the fact that it is often "invisible" work. The federal sector's efforts don't have the visibility of the private sector—which uses mass media to single out star performers and successful organizations—and employees are apt not to be perceived as interesting or as active in their field. Because the relationship of the federal budget to income taxes is always a subject of public debate, federal employees are seen by some as a burden on the tax rate. On the other hand, recent events have made the public more open to seeing the benefits of having a strong, organized federal government, particularly when it comes to issues such as national defense.

The Right Qualifications

Let's examine the government classification of sociologist (GS-184) as a good example of what training and qualifications are expected of an entry-level federal employee in this field.

Description of the Work. Sociologists employ established sociological methods and techniques to perform work that relates to (1) the culture, structure, or functioning of groups, organizations, or social systems; (2) the relationships between groups, organizations, or social systems; (3) collective human behavior in social situations; and (4) the demographic characteristics and ecological patterning of communities and societies. The work requires a professional knowledge of sociology, sociological theory, and methods of social research. Sociologists also interpret research results, articulate the implications of research for policy, and administer programs making use of research results.

Basic Requirements of All Grades. Candidates for all positions must have successfully completed at least one of the following basic requirements.

• A four-year program in an accredited college or university leading to a bachelor's degree or higher that includes or is supplemented by at least twenty-four credit hours of sociology, with course work including the theory and methods of social research.

• Courses in an accredited college or university consisting of twenty-four semester hours in sociology, with course work including the theory and methods of social research, plus additional experience or education. This combination will total four years of education and experience and give the applicant a technical knowledge comparable to that described in the first point.

While the specifications for sociologist require a sociology degree, as previously noted, the OPM has categorized a number of jobs that are open to any qualified graduate with a four-year degree. This includes positions such as environmental protection specialist (GS-028), budget analyst (GS-560), archives specialist (GS-1421), administrative officer (GS-341), manpower developer (GS-142), and many, many others.

Even for those positions requiring a four-year degree, a generous range of degrees is frequently acceptable. In Chapter 7, you read of numerous opportunities for using your degree in the human resources management function of private businesses and organizations. These same jobs exist in the federal government. For example, the entire range of human resources officers (GS-200, including specialist level positions in personnel management, personnel staffing, salary and wage administration, employee relations, labor relations, and employee development) requires a four-year degree from an accredited college or university, the ability to communicate effectively both orally and in writing, analytical ability, and a general understanding of the system and methods and administrative machinery that accomplishes the work of any organization.

Earnings

Job security and competitive pay are among the top attractions for many seeking federal employment. There are eight predominant pay systems. Approximately half of the workforce is under the General Schedule (GS) pay scale, 20 percent are paid under the Postal Service rates, and about 10 percent are paid under the Prevailing Rate Schedule Wage Grade (WG) Classification. The additional pay systems include the Executive Schedule, Foreign Service,

Nonappropriated Fund Instrumentalities scales, and Veterans Health Administration.

While the private sector offers higher salaries for some specialized positions, particularly in fields such as medicine, engineering, and computer technology, government salaries are still considered competitive. One of the more welcome aspects of a government job is that pay raises, advancement, and promotion is determined by largely objective criteria, and your ability to grow in your career and be rewarded for that growth is explicitly outlined. Benefits and pension plans are competitive and, in some work situations, unique.

The most common federal pay scale you will encounter is the GS. Jobs for entry-level college graduates usually are at GS-5 or GS-7. Promotion is usually two grades at once until GS-11; at that point, each promotion results in one grade at a time. Within each grade are steps; these within-grade increases occur based on time on the job. Most people start at Step 1 of their GS grade level. For some kinds of positions (especially those in short supply), there are higher salaries, and for some locations (Los Angeles, New York City, San Francisco), cost-of-living differentials are added to the base salary.

The chart on page 176 shows the GS Salaries as of January 1, 2008.

Career Outlook

Generally, federal employment is not as severely affected by cyclical fluctuations in the economy as is employment in many private sector industries, such as construction and manufacturing. However, shifting national priorities and concerns can have a dramatic effect on staffing levels. Each presidential administration may have different public policy priorities that result in greater levels of federal employment in some programs and declines in others. Layoffs, also called reductions in force, have occurred in the past; however, they are uncommon and generally affect relatively few workers. Some extraordinary circumstances, such as military engagement, will also affect the number of people hired by the federal government.

On the whole, however, employment in the federal government remains relatively stable over the course of time. It is a particularly appealing field for entry-level workers, especially because promotion to senior positions is generally done with existing staff. The opportunities for those hoping to enter the public forces at a more senior level will depend on whether they can bring to the table particular skills that are in short supply within the existing government ranks.

Although entry-level employment remains the best start to a federal career, it is good to remember that the government is a very competitive

Grade	Step 1	Step 2	Step 3	Step 4	Step 5	Step 6	Step 7	Step 8	Step 9	Step 10	Within Grade Amounts
1	17,046	17,615	18,182	18,746	19,313	19,646	20,206	20,771	20,793	21,324	Varies
2	19,165	19,621	20,255	20,793	21,025	21,643	22,261	22,879	23,497	24,115	Varies
3	20,911	21,608	22,305	23,002	23,699	24,396	25,093	25,790	26,487	27,184	697
4	23,475	24,258	25,041	25,824	26,607	27,390	28,173	28,956	29,739	30,522	783
5	26,264	27,139	28,014	28,889	29,764	30,639	34,514	32,389	33,264	34,139	875
6	29,276	30,252	31,228	32,204	33,180	34,156	35,132	36,108	37,084	38,060	976
7	32,534	33,618	34,702	35,786	36,870	37,954	39,038	40,122	41,206	42,290	1,084
8	36,030	37,231	37,432	39,633	40,834	42,035	43,236	44,437	45,638	46,839	1,201
9	39,795	41,122	42,449	43,776	45,103	46,430	47,757	49,084	50,411	51,738	1,327
10	43,824	45,285	46,746	48,207	49,668	51,129	52,590	54,051	55,512	56,973	1,461
11	48,148	49,753	51,358	52,963	54,568	56,173	57,778	59,383	60,988	62,593	1,605
12	57,709	59,633	651,557	63,481	65,405	67,329	69,253	71,177	73,101	75,025	1,924
13	68,625	70,913	73,201	75,489	77,777	80,065	82,353	84,641	86,929	89,217	2,288
14	81,093	83,796	86,499	89,202	91,905	94,608	97,311	100,014	102,717	105,420	2,703
15	95,390	98,570	101,750	104,930	108,110	111,290	114,470	117,650	120,830	124,010	3,108

employer whose labor force by all standards is better educated and more technically astute with higher language and math skills than the workforce as a whole. In spite of the number of positions available to any four-year graduate, those individuals with scientific, computer, and other quantitative skills definitely have an edge over others.

As a sociology major considering a governmental position, you can look at jobs that value your specific degree. If you want to enhance your attractiveness as a job candidate for a federal position, however, you might consider acquiring some additional and more technical skills while in college. Take advantage of courses such as Statistics or Research Design. These would make an impressive addition to your degree. Or enroll in some advanced computer courses, such as Systems Design or Information Technology. Talk to a computer science adviser about what two or three courses would work well together for you as a nonmajor.

These are simply two possible options that will enhance your attractiveness to a federal hiring agency. Experience is also important. If you can document some related work experience, you are not only more competitive but also entering the government workforce at a higher scale.

Strategy for Finding Federal Jobs

Before doing anything else, identify the federal job titles that are right for your combination of education and experience. Candidates for federal jobs must apply for specific job titles. At any given time, the government is hiring for just about every position, so the best way to learn exactly what job titles you want to apply for is to look and see what positions are open. On the OPM's USAJOBS website, you can search for job openings (which contain detailed job descriptions) under a number of categories, including professional, entry-level professional, clerical and technician, and worker-trainee. Say you were to begin your search with entry-level professional positions. You would then be able to narrow it down by field, such as social science and welfare or medical and health. Other job/career sites provide similar information; just browse around.

As noted earlier, the OPM has moved toward a web-based hiring process, and several agencies (such as the EPA) will only accept applications submitted online. It is expected that in the coming years this trend will only increase, hence it is in your interests to become familiar with the online application process. It is important to find out whether you are to apply through the OPM or directly with the particular agency. The careers section on federal Web pages will assist you in determining the proper route of application. You will need to identify the position and submit an application that contains the particular job title and announcement number.

As might be expected, each job application will have different require-ments, depending on the level, agency, and location. Thus it is not possible to submit a one-size-fits-all application for government jobs, just as you would not be able to in the private sector. Instead, pay close attention to the specific requests for information required for each position you are apply-ing for.

Once your application has been processed through the preliminary stages, you will have a formal job interview. There may also be examinations or tests to fulfill the skills requirements for any given position.

The end result—obtaining one of the many excellent government jobs for individuals with sociology degrees—more than justifies the means. Admit-tedly, the process includes a challenging and sometimes frustratingly detailed and complex set of job postings, applications, and hiring rules and regula-tions. It can become a job in itself just to master the various systems. Remem-ber that the government, whether it be federal, state, or local, is made up of millions of people just like you. They are interested in your application. So if the going gets tough, and it probably will, ask for help.

Contact the Department Directly. Successful governmental job seekers have indicated that one of the best ways to break through the bureaucracy is to personalize it. Even though the application process is increasingly com-puterized, this does not preclude speaking with human resources represen-tatives in various agencies. You will also find that most of the individual websites of different government departments contain very informative sec-tions on seeking a career with that agency. There you will find contact names and numbers, as well as helpful hints for creating a successful application.

Review All Federal Job Sources. The government job market is unlike any other. Consequently, your job-search strategies will be different as well. Your first task will be to make certain that you are seeing as many of the avail-able job postings as you can. While the OPM's USAJOBS site is by far the largest listing of federal job openings, other sites can help you narrow your search or suggest other routes to follow. Make sure to check each of the rel-evant sources. You will become familiar with each source and determine how often new jobs are listed so that you can create a postings review schedule for yourself.

Try as many of the services that follow as your time and budget allow. One excellent place to start is with the Federal Jobs Digest Matching Service, which offers shortcuts in the long process of identifying where you would find your best government job fit. The government job sites are free to use.

Federal Jobs Digest Matching Service
Federal Jobs Digest
326 Main Street
Emmaus, PA 10591
jobsfed.com

This service matches your background to federal requirements. You send in a copy of your résumé (either by e-mail or regular mail) and receive a list of job titles and grade levels for which you qualify. Federal job descriptions and qualification statements are provided for every job title that the service identifies for you. The fee for the service is $35. Use the information to streamline your job search using the federal application channels.

Office of Personnel Management. The OPM is the source of employment and listings for many federal government positions, but with decentralization, many agencies and departments can hire independently. The OPM remains the best source on the application process for government jobs in general. Along with the USAJOBS website (usajobs.opm.gov), the OPM also runs an automated telephone system that allows you to access information on current job openings.

Studentjobs.gov. This is a joint project between the OPM and the U.S. Department of Education's Student Financial Assistance Office. Most federal agencies post their openings on this website, including positions that are available to you while you are still in college or graduate school. This resource also provides a "gateway" to agencies that are hiring. Check it out at studentjobs.gov.

Potential Employers
Agencies hiring the largest numbers of college graduates (any degree) include the departments of Health and Human Services, Veterans Affairs, Housing and Urban Development (HUD), Defense, Agriculture, Interior, Commerce, Transportation, Education, and Energy. College graduates may also find work in special government agencies such as the Peace Corps, the National Institutes of Health (NIH), and the National Institute on Aging. Each governmental unit has its own human resources department, and you would be best advised to directly contact the ones you would like to work for. The following is a list of several federal agencies that might be of interest to sociology majors. Be advised that federal government addresses change with remarkable frequency, so it is best to check on the website of a particular agency to get the correct and up-to-date contact information.

- Administration for Children and Families: acf.hhs.gov/children
- Administration on Aging: aoa.gov
- Bureau of Prisons: bop.gov
- Bureau of the Census: census.gov
- Centers for Disease Control and Prevention: cdc.gov
- Commission on Civil Rights: usccr.gov
- Department of Agriculture: usda.gov
- Department of Commerce: doc.gov
- Department of Defense: defenselink.mil
- Department of Education: ed.gov
- Department of Energy: energy.gov
- Department of Health and Human Services: hhs.gov
- Department of Justice: usdoj.gov
- Department of State: state.gov
- Department of Transportation: dot.gov
- Department of Veterans Affairs: va.gov
- Drug Enforcement Administration: dea.gov
- Environmental Protection Agency: epa.gov
- National Institutes of Health: nih.gov
- Peace Corps: peacecorps.gov

For a complete list of Canadian government agencies, including links to each agency or department, go to gc.ca/depts/major/depind-eng.html.

Possible Job Titles

When investigating government jobs, it's a good idea to create your own customized list of job titles for each sector of public employment. In so doing, you may be surprised and gratified at the range of job titles that your sociology degree qualifies you to fill. There is almost no limit to your options once you step into the public sector. In addition to the possibilities mentioned earlier in the chapter, the following titles will get you started thinking about the spectrum of choices before you.

Academic exchange specialist
Customs inspector
Employee development specialist
Human rights worker
Intelligence research specialist
Labor and employee relations specialist

Legislative aide
Peace Corps volunteer
Position classification specialist

State, Provincial, and Local Government

When people consider a job in government, they often overlook the rich source of options available at the state, provincial, and local levels. But it is at these levels that some of the more engaging and fulfilling work is to be found, bringing your background in sociology to bear on the issues affecting your own community. For example, a large city government working to resuscitate its downtown area may desire someone with sociology experience to help develop trade and to market the attractiveness of housing possibilities in the center city. A state economic development office seeking industry to locate within their boundaries might develop a task force to identify potential workers to attract new industry. The individual who brings a knowledge of sociology to these kinds of teams provides an irreplaceable service.

The need for workers with sociology skills has become much more pronounced at all levels of civil service employment, including states, provinces, cities, towns, and municipalities. Police officers even in midsized cities, for example, may find growing communities of people whose principal language is not English. These communities have a structure and value system that needs a sociology graduate's sensitivity and education to communicate to others who may not understand their neighbors.

State and Provincial Government

With the exception of foreign policy and defense, state and provincial jobs mimic the federal level to a remarkable degree. Finding a job with state or provincial governments is similar to finding one with the federal government. Depending on the size of the state and the bureaucracy established, the system may be as complex and multitiered as the federal government. Unlike the federal government, however, there is apt to be a central personnel office (usually in the capitol) and branch personnel offices that list all openings and can provide specifications sheets for each of these positions. These spec sheets list required qualifications and salary schedules and tell you whether a test is part of the application process.

State and provincial governments have become increasingly professionalized; consequently, competition for positions is keen and the candidates are often exceptional. While local governments emphasize elementary and secondary education, health, and police and fire services, state governments emphasize higher education, health, highway, and correctional services.

Visit a state or provincial human resources office, learn how to file a formal application, and read the current job postings. Stay abreast of additional postings by Internet, fax, phone, or periodic visits. In some states, you can file one application and indicate the kinds of jobs you want to be considered for. Your application will become part of those applicant pools for a period of time.

If you know where you want to work in state or provincial government, visit that location, meet the people associated with the office, and express your interest. Bring a résumé or arrange for an informational interview (see Part One). However, a word of caution is due here. This is best done ahead of any formal job posting. To make such a visit after a job is announced would be disadvantageous for you and uncomfortable and anxiety provoking for personnel in the state office.

The state human resources office can be of great assistance in explaining the various state agencies and directing you to more information about the mission of each of them. Remember, their job is to secure the best qualified applicants, so they're interested in raising your level of awareness and appreciation of state government.

Local Government

There are thousands of government and public sector agencies throughout the United States and Canada. Many of them not only fit your sociology degree in the kinds of jobs available, but also represent a promising employment market.

Many different local government institutions make up the crazy patchwork quilt of democracy in the United States and Canada, and you will need to conduct your own research on the who, where, and what of each local governmental unit to understand them. Fortunately, most local government jobs are advertised and communicated to the general public.

Typically, you will be looking at five categories of employers in local government:

1. Counties: Used as a local unit of government throughout the United States except in Connecticut, Rhode Island, and the District of Columbia.
2. Municipalities: Called cities, towns, villages, or boroughs, these urban areas incorporated within or sometimes separate from their resident county function as governmental units on their own.

3. Townships: A political subdivision of a county found in twenty states in the eastern and midwestern part of the United States, they can be called *towns*, *plantations*, or *locations* and are governed by elected boards.
4. School Districts: Existing both dependently and independently, these are found in an overwhelming majority of states (except Virginia, Maryland, North Carolina, Hawaii, Alaska, and the District of Columbia) to administer school systems.
5. Special Districts: Otherwise termed *boards*, *authorities*, or *commissions*, these government units often focus on only one service. They administer services such as cemeteries, water, sewage, fire protection, parks and recreation, flood control, highways, and libraries.

Nowhere will your curiosity, perseverance, and research skills serve you better than in your exploration of jobs in local governments. Unlike the federal and state systems, local governments conform to no overall system. Each is different, and informal aspects of the job search (talking directly to local officials) may be far more important than the formal application process.

The composition, names of offices, and structure of these various governing organizations is idiosyncratic. The different structures have evolved over time, and the only similarities tend to be in the functions of local government. Typical functions include education, health care, highway maintenance, police, fire, parks and recreation, sewage, and water quality.

There is no one strategy for approaching this diversity of local government organizations. Some small towns' hiring practices are very informal, and a résumé, letter, and request for a formal interview might actually disqualify you. Other governmental organizations have job postings, application processes, and pay-scale systems that rival their federal and state counterparts.

You must assess each local government structure individually and decide on your best approach. Once again, share what you are looking for with people, ask lots of questions, and use local reference sources (such as the local library and their staff) to educate yourself on the kinds of jobs available, what it might take to fill them, and the type of application process used.

Strategy for Finding State, Provincial, and Local Jobs

Where are the jobs? As you've seen in the discussion on federal job sources, knowledge is power, and the federal government, for all its complexity, is manageable. State, provincial, and local government jobs can be found through national, regional, and local sources. State and local government jobs are grouped together here because many of the sources combine these two categories. Your very best bet for state or provincial government jobs is the state or provincial employment office and its branches, which produce job listings and specification sheets for all state or provincial government positions. Your college career office may be on a mailing list for state or provincial job listings. Both state or provincial and local jobs are also advertised regionally in the want-ad section of the newspaper.

One of your easiest sources of job listings to access is the telephone directory. Many county, city, and state human resources offices maintain an employment hotline or employment information job line. And it should be no surprise that many local governments post information regarding job openings on their websites. Check the telephone book under the particular governmental unit and call the number. Or use the websites of state, provincial, or local government agencies to identify job openings and key contacts. Resources such as *Government Jobs in America*, *Government Job Finder*, and *Careers in Nonprofits and Government Agencies* can also be helpful.

Paperwork Is Critical. The application and hiring process in public employment is often more heavily dependent, in the early stages, on the careful submission of paperwork. As a recent college graduate, you would have the advantage of on-campus recruiting, numerous job postings in your career office, and many posters and fliers from hiring organizations eager to interview new college graduates. Although public employment relies more heavily on application forms and résumés to initially screen their applicants, once the interview process is initiated there is little difference between public and private employment screening.

Knowing this, you should appreciate the importance of paying particular attention to the application forms and their completion, whether in electronic form or "hard copy." Many application forms demand frustratingly long responses in very small spaces, often requiring attaching additional sheets. You will want to make several copies of each form and work out your responses on a copy of your original form before completing the finished product. Appearance is critical, as is the thoroughness of your information.

Follow-Up. The people who staff offices in the public sector are no different from anyone else; they are just people. Once you have applied for a position and your paperwork is complete, don't be shy about telephoning, stopping in, or writing a brief note to inquire about your application or the hiring process for the position you are seeking. Applicants frequently say, "But, I don't want to be a pest!" Unless someone specifically tells you that your contact is inappropriate or unnecessary, maintain a professionally active interest in the position you are seeking. It is just as important to follow up on your government application as it is in the private sector. Make contact to verify that your materials were received, to demonstrate that you are actively involved in your job search, or simply to remind them of your qualifications and availability for employment. If you have not yet visited the office or agency you would like to work for, and you are able to do so, now is the time to put a face with one of the many applications that these offices receive. Introduce yourself, check on the status of your application, and let them see your energy and enthusiasm.

The incorrect impression is that jobs in the government sector undergo a more impersonal, formalized screening process than a similar search in the private sector. Because of the highly structured classification of employees in government, most applicants believe that once you submit your application, there is little you can do but wait out the process.

The reality is that for anyone who is responsible for a hiring decision, the ultimate goal is the same—the best person for the job. While public sector employment application processes and hiring conditions are certainly more codified than in the private sector, that does not mean you cannot put a face to your application or a voice to your name with a visit or a phone call.

Potential Employers

You will need some strategy to build your list of possible employers in the specific state, provincial, or local government units you may be considering for your job search. State or provincial human resources offices may list jobs, but you'll want to contact the hiring departments directly. For a local government search, you will need to build your own personal directory of the local hiring authorities. For a national search of local government jobs, consult the websites of state, provincial, or local government agencies in which you might be interested.

Many smaller municipalities will not and cannot afford to mail job listings. If such information is not available online, offer to send some self-addressed, stamped envelopes if cost is the objection. Some state offices will maintain limited mailing lists; others may require you to visit a human resources office or satellite location in person to pick up job listings. Some maintain telephone job lines that list that week's vacancies in a recording, updated weekly. In your initial contact with any employment office, ask about these options so that you can stay abreast of current offerings.

Possible Job Titles

Following are possible job titles you may find in state or provincial government jobs:

Administrative assistant
Affirmative action worker
Analyst
Assistant director
Assistant manager
Inspector
Investigator
Personnel coordinator
Program aid
Program assistant
Program coordinator
Program monitor
Supervisor

The following job titles may be found at the local level:

Administrative analyst
Administrative assistant
Corrections staffer
Counselor
Investigator
Inspector
Juvenile court worker
Office manager
Planner
Program analyst
Program planner
Rehabilitation counselor
Urban planner

Professional Associations

If you're not sure what type of governmental work you want to seek, review the following list of government-related associations to get an idea of what the possibilities are.

Alliance for Nonprofit Management
1899 L Street NW, 6th Floor
Washington, DC 20036
allianceonline.org
Members/Purpose: Seeks to further education and leadership capabilities to enhance both individuals and the management of the nonprofit organization.
Publications: *Alliance Insights*, conference reports, *Gold Book*, reports and studies
Training: Provides opportunity to further education through information sharing and networking among members
Job Listings: Offers online CareerBank

American Federation of State, County and Municipal Employees (AFSCME)
1625 L Street NW
Washington, DC 20036
afscme.org
Members/Purpose: Represents 1.4 million public service employees.
Publications: *AFSCME Works Magazine*, *Prime Time* newsletter, other print publications and Web documents
Training: Offers training in political action, public speaking, and other areas
Job Listings: Posts job openings online

American Foreign Service Association (AFSA)
2101 E Street NW
Washington, DC 20037
afsa.org
Members/Purpose: Associate membership is open to individuals and international organizations and corporations interested in foreign affairs, international trade, and economic policy.
Publications: *Foreign Service Journal*, *AFSA News*, directory of members, e-mail updates
Training: Conducts international conferences and symposia
Job Listings: Website provides links to openings in federal agencies

Association of Inspectors General
Historic Carpenters' Hall
320 Chestnut Street
Philadelphia, PA 19106
inspectorsgeneral.org

Members/Purpose: Consists of inspectors general and professional staff in their agencies, as well as other officials responsible for inspection and oversight with respect to public, not-for-profit, and independent sector organizations.
Publications: Newsletter
Training: Sponsors conferences
Job Listings: None

BoardSource
1828 L Street NW, Suite 900
Washington, DC 20036-5114
boardsource.org
Members/Purpose: Building effective nonprofit boards. Seeks to improve the effectiveness of nonprofit organizations in fields such as arts and culture, conservation, religion, youth development, public policy, health and medicine, and social welfare by strengthening their governing boards.
Publications: *Board Member* magazine, e-newsletter, books and booklets
Training: Offers assistance in organizing training programs, workshops, and seminars for nonprofit organizations
Job Listings: None

Civil Service Employees Association (CSEA)
143 Washington Avenue
Albany, NY 12210
csealocal1000.org
Members/Purpose: AFL-CIO. Members are state and local government employees from all public employee classifications.
Publications: Newsletter, *Public Sector*
Training: Conducts training and education programs in labor education
Job Listings: Offers career development assistance; website includes links to job opportunities

Federal Managers Association (FMA)
1641 Prince Street
Alexandria, VA 22314-2818
fedmanagers.org
Members/Purpose: Advocates excellence in public service; serves nearly two hundred thousand government managers and executives.

Publications: *The Federal Manager*, *The Washington Report*
Training: Sponsors Federal Management Institute; holds conferences
Job Listings: None

Government Finance Officers Association of U.S. and Canada (GFOA)
203 North LaSalle Street, Suite 2700
Chicago, IL 60601-1210
gfoa.org
Members/Purpose: Finance officers from city, county, state, provincial, and
    federal governments, schools, and other special districts; retirement
    systems, colleges, universities, public accounting firms, financial
    institutions, and others in the United States and Canada interested in
    government finance.
Publications: *Government Finance Review*, newsletter, membership
    directory, reports and studies
Training: Sponsors Government Finance Institute; holds conferences and
    seminars
Job Listings: Lists job openings online

International City/County Management Association (ICMA)
777 North Capitol Street NE, Suite 500
Washington, DC 20002-4201
icma.org
Members/Purpose: International professional and educational organization
    for appointed administrators and assistant administrators serving cities,
    counties, districts, and regions.
Publications: *ICMA Newsletter*, *Public Management Magazine*, membership
    directory, e-library of publications
Training: Operates ICMA Training Institute
Job Listings: Job Opportunities Bulletin

National Association of Government Communicators (NAGC)
201 Park Washington Court
Falls Church, VA 22046
Members/Purpose: Government employees, retired persons, nongovern-
    ment affiliates, and students. Seeks to advance communications as an
    essential professional resource at every level of national, state, and local
    government.
Publications: *NAGC Communicator*

Training: Holds conferences and workshops; offers communications training

Job Listings: Maintains placement service; posts job openings online

National Association of Government Employees (NAGE)
159 Burgin Parkway
Quincy, MA 02169
nage.org

Members/Purpose: Union of civilian federal government employees and members in military agencies, Internal Revenue Service, Post Office, Veterans Administration, General Services Administration, Federal Aviation Administration, and other federal agencies, as well as in state and local agencies.

Publications: *The Fednews*

Training: Offers seminars

Job Listings: None

National Association of Governmental Labor Officials (NAGLO)
2760 Research Park Drive
Lexington, KY 40511
naglo.org

Members/Purpose: Elected and appointed heads of state labor departments. Seeks to assist labor officials in performing their duties and to improve employment conditions for American workers.

Publications: *NAGLO Update, State Labor Directory*

Training: Sponsors conferences

Job Listings: None

National Association of Regional Councils (NARC)
1666 Connecticut Avenue NW, Suite 300
Washington, DC 20009
narc.org

Members/Purpose: Interested in regionalism as an approach to meeting problems that cross local governmental boundaries, including economic development, transportation, environmental management, housing, services to the elderly, and rural development.

Publications: Directory, newsletter, special reports

Training: Holds conventions and meetings; sponsors Regional Futures Institute

Job Listings: Lists job openings online

National Organization of Black County Officials (NOBCO)
1090 Vermont Avenue NW
Washington, DC 20005
nobcoinc.org
Members/Purpose: Black county officials organized to provide program
    planning and management assistance to selected counties in the United
    States. Acts as a technical information exchange to develop resolutions to
    problems on the local and national levels.
Publications: *County Compass* (quarterly), *County to County* (bimonthly)
Training: Conducts seminars
Job Listings: None

Society of Government Meeting Professionals (SGMP)
908 King Street
Alexandria, VA 22314
sgmp.org
Members/Purpose: Individuals involved in planning government meetings
    on a full- or part-time basis; suppliers of services to government
    planners. Provides education in basic and advanced areas of meeting
    planning and facilities; professional contact with other government
    planners and suppliers knowledgeable in government contracting.
Publications: *Advantage Magazine, Government Meeting Professional*
    newsletter, membership directory
Training: Holds regional and national conferences; sponsors certification
    programs; operates the Gilmer Institute of Learning
Job Listings: None

Society for Nonprofit Organizations (SNPO)
5820 Canton Center Road, Suite 165
Canton, MI 48187
snpo.org
Members/Purpose: Executive directors, staff, board members, volunteers,
    and other professionals who serve nonprofit organizations.
Publications: *Nonprofit World, National Directory of Service/Product
    Providers, Funding Alert*
Training: Sponsors seminars and workshops on nonprofit management and
    leadership
Job Listings: Offers online job information

Path 5:
Social Research and
Data Analysis

Some sociology graduates find themselves specializing in research and analysis. For example, picture yourself working as an entry-level researcher at an organization that is engaged in exploring drug use and related violence in the population of rural American teenagers. Your place of employment is funded by government and foundation grants; it has just received a grant from the Substance Abuse and Mental Health Services Administration to gather information about which drugs are most readily available to teenagers outside of big cities, who is doing the selling, and where narcotics are being sold.

This type of research request, even though it might sound simple, involves significant effort. Historical analysis of police logs and arrest records over many years with subjects categorized by age, family structure, educational history, juvenile justice records, and other categories will probably be required. All this information will need to be entered into databases so that you can run correlations and analyses that will provide insight into the issues.

In this effort, your research might involve many nights as a participant observer, riding through dark roads in the backseat of a patrol car to observe drug trafficking at close hand. You may accompany police officers to drug houses, observe a bust, and watch suspects being arrested and handcuffed. Your study might involve actual interviews with criminal suspects and with members of the police force.

Perhaps surprisingly, a career in social research and data analysis can involve a great deal of action. It is not dull, it is not a desk job, and it is not dry and dusty. It is highly social, can be very exciting, and has even been dangerous for some researchers. And it is vital to our understanding of social patterns.

To understand different forms of social behavior, researchers use a variety of methods, procedures, and research strategies. Usually the research project begins with a definition of the problem and areas to be studied. Then all the different factors or variables must be identified and any relationships between variables expressed. Sometimes the relationship between two variables is only a generalization that must be studied to be proved empirically. Those generalizations of relationships are called hypotheses.

Sociological research can take place in the laboratory or in the field; it can be done by surveys or studies. Every research strategy has its advantages and disadvantages in terms of cost, time commitment, and the precision possible with any particular technique.

Different Focus Areas

The different focus areas that might be addressed by sociological researchers offer a great deal of variety. For instance, research on family support programs is certainly worthwhile work, and the results of your research efforts may have broad implications. Although much social research has public approval, some may be more controversial. In addition, some research methods may be seen as violating people's privacy.

Ethical issues are critical for the researcher in sociology because social research is about people's lives. Most gathering of data presents some ethical issues for the researcher, not only relating to the methods but sometimes about the implications of the findings. Frequently, controversy over social research has centered around the applications of the research as well as the means by which data are obtained. If you are considering a career in applied research, especially in government and business, you may confront ethical questions about the kinds of studies being undertaken and the uses to which the data are being put.

Research careers in sociology generally come in a close second in popularity to teaching careers for those with a master's degree or doctorate. In fact, for those who go on to advanced degrees in sociology, teaching and research go hand in hand. Research is one of the common core career options suggested by the American Sociological Association for those holding at least a master's degree in sociology.

The research and data analysis careers discussed in this chapter are specifically those available in the private sector to the bachelor's degree candidate. Public agencies at the federal, state, and local level also provide a number of fine research jobs. Most of the applied research positions that will be discussed in this chapter are equally available in the public sector. For example, the position of legislative aide is frequently a research position, designing and executing studies for lawmakers or gathering and interpreting existing secondary data.

Private corporations, research institutes, nonprofit agencies, and, of course, businesses are all big users of research services. Much of the research done by these organizations concerns people and how they behave. If the organization is large enough and the research department well funded, you will find a level of professionalism that could well provide a springboard to further education and enhanced job opportunities.

The types of jobs in this career path require that you truly enjoy the research process and all that it entails; you need to enjoy problems and problem solving. In your own self-assessment process, you may have realized that you enjoy challenges and are creative in not only seeing these challenges from different perspectives, but in solving them as well. That would be an important attribute to anyone contemplating a career in research or data analysis.

While problem solving and critical thinking are easily recognized as requirements in this area, good writing skills are also essential. Outlining research projects and expressing the relationships between variables, hypotheses, or findings requires an extensive vocabulary and a sense of style and nuance. "Elegant" is an adjective frequently used to describe not only the design of a research study but also the expression of the data in the written word. Writing facility will become even more critical as you seek to advance your career.

Rapidly advancing technology, principally in terms of computer and communications capabilities, has accelerated not only the quantity and detail of information, but also the speed at which we can provide information to those needing it. Sociologists and those researching in sociology depend heavily on the computer for just that reason. However, computers demand precision and quality. Anyone who has struggled to write even the most basic program can appreciate the painstakingly simple logic of the computer, which when accelerated and provided with multiple tasks and huge amounts of information, becomes truly awesome.

While most jobs in this career path require significant computer skills, the everyday world of the sociologist is most often uncertain, illogical, and highly qualitative. Computers and information processing, in general, introduce a strong bias toward producing and using information and criteria that may even contradict the realities they are intended to deal with.

Sociology provides so many different ways to look at the world and to rethink how we understand social life, change, and the causes and consequences of human behavior. It offers a range of research techniques from participant observation, experimental studies (both in and out of the laboratory), surveys, and field studies. These can be applied to any issue from street crime to mainstreaming and learning disabilities to consumers' perceptions of competing products. The research function is an exciting discipline with enormous opportunities and a wide range of career paths.

Definition of the Career Path

Some people might believe that research and data analysis positions are dead-end jobs. But they actually can provide great starting points for other types of related work, as well as be rewarding jobs in themselves.

Here's just one example. Perhaps you leave college and take a position as research assistant with a small manufacturer in your state. You work hard (of course) and, after a few years of experience and some success, you are promoted to an associate position in the department. At this point, you would be in a particularly good position to move to another organization as a data analysis manager or database manager or, if the organization was large enough, to a position as associate or assistant director of research.

If changing organizations doesn't appeal to you, you might find opportunities for growth right at your doorstep. Perhaps you can provide your manufacturing firm with enough evidence of the effect of your research on sales, profitability, and consumer satisfaction to warrant a larger expenditure on research activities. You are given more space, more financial resources, and even, perhaps, the directorship of a new department—research! At about this time in your career, you may also be receiving strong signals from your professional colleagues or mentors that you need to continue your education to remain eligible for promotion.

The Working Environment

A common assumption about careers in research and data analysis is that they are "behind-the-scenes" jobs or, even more incorrectly, desk jobs. Nothing could be farther from the truth. The variety and descriptions of the research and data analyst positions cited in this chapter should be your first indications that these are active, vital, involved positions that require energy, enthusiasm, curiosity, and, sometimes, good driving skills.

Researchers in sociology and sociologically related fields are not brought on board after a project is designed or up and running. They participate in the original thinking of any project and in every stage of project design and implementation.

Important aspects of research or data analyst positions with a bachelor's degree include:

- Collaboration
- Networking
- Customer service orientation
- Balancing multiple projects
- Supervision

The Collaborative Angle

No doubt about it: research is demanding. Anyone working in research will tell you that even the simplest projects can consume many hours of work in planning, data gathering, and report writing. They will also tell you research is not just "done." Research is conducted for a purpose. Someone has asked a question or postulated a theory that needs evidence to formulate a response.

Many roles are involved in a research team. Some people on your team will design the research project, stipulating the data-gathering techniques; others will design the necessary instruments (surveys, experiments); and still others will collect the information that is passed on for others to organize and enter. Some team members will analyze that information, while others will write the research findings. Yet another group may present those findings before an audience. Researchers and data analysts are an important and integral part of any project team and are included from the beginning stages of any project.

High-level involvement may come as a surprise to some who are unaware of the active role researchers and data analysts play, not only in providing support for planning needs but in helping to shape strategy. Knowledge of the organization's past experiences, successes, and failures and an ability to bring those experiences to bear on new efforts makes the information specialists important team players, and not just behind-the-scenes resources.

Networking

Misconceptions about researchers continue to persist. One is that researchers are always solitary. Another is that researchers and analysts are "keepers" of information. Both of these ideas are incorrect. Research can be a very social process that relies on extensive networks of professional relationships that can help you secure the information you need quickly and efficiently. Researchers are not interested in hoarding what they learn but want to share it with others. Many researchers voluntarily send ideas, information, articles, and relevant materials to individuals they know have an interest. Of course, owing to your own innate sense of organization as a researcher, you will build some files of your own. This may help you respond to frequent requests for the same kind of information. But you can never acquire all the information you need for a project ahead of time. You will have to generate the research you need for a project through your own efforts combined with those of your contacts and whatever networks you develop.

Networking can be a specific job demand, or it can be a skill you need to develop to secure the information you are seeking. In providing a historical analysis of window curtain treatments over the past ten years to determine trends in window dressing for a curtain manufacturer, you may first seek historical sales figures from the sales division and then rely on your computer department for processing and printing that data. You may do some research outside the organization on competitors' sales and employ the services of a librarian or commercial data-retrieval firm. You may go to a library yourself to read and view advertisements in older magazines. You might watch videotapes of popular television shows to observe how window treatments were designed to reflect the model families of decades past. Very often your work is the product of cooperation among many individuals, and information specialists maintain elaborate and well-developed networks of contacts to provide them with the information they need.

Customer Service Research

Despite its analytical underpinnings, research is in many ways a "people business." So the researcher needs to respond to clients (customers) in a positive, service-oriented, and professional manner. Research and data analysis is crucial to many projects. So get ready to be popular and busy! To have fun doing this, you need to understand that you are the specialist in information, and those seeking your help are your customers. They can't always appreciate the work behind their requests or even, sometimes, the feasibility of providing the information they want. You'll enjoy your job a great deal more if you can avoid getting angry or frustrated that people don't understand everything that's involved in what you do. Just remember that the woman or man who can provide on-target information when it's needed is going to be a vital member of any organization. You'll be even more prized if you can provide that information quickly and in a manner that people can appreciate and understand without being burdened with all the technicalities involved in accessing it.

Don't be surprised to hear speed mentioned in a research job. A common complaint of both researchers and data analysts is that "everybody wants it yesterday." Fortunately, many requests repeat themselves with stunning regularity, and the skillful resource professional will build information packets to satisfy those traditional requests. But many searches are challenging and are prompted by a need to respond to some outside influence or market demand—quickly! If you begin with a clear and mutually agreed-upon definition of the materials and information requested, you have accomplished the most important element in rapid information provision. A good staff, the right technology, a strong memory, developed note-taking skills, and efficient records management and retrieval will all help you to get information seekers what they need as quickly as possible.

In an information management position, you have the opportunity to meet and help coworkers from every department and level of employment within your organization. You'll be called on frequently, not just for formal requests for information but for the simple questions, such as "How many employees did we have in 1955?" or "Where exactly in the city was our first showroom?" As an information resource professional, you will very often (and wisely) be brought in early in the planning stages of most projects so that you have a full understanding of the information needs of all concerned parties. This helps you to best consider how to accomplish the task.

Frequently, you'll get requests for information that you don't understand. The person making the request may be unused to dealing with an information specialist and not particularly adept at expressing informational needs. That's where your communication skills and customer service orientation come into play. Skillful questioning and a patient manner with good eye contact and attending behavior will encourage people to express exactly what they perceive to be their requests. Your questions and discussion will help clarify the request and bring your results closer to their original intentions.

Supervision

The official title of sociologist is reserved for those individuals with advanced degrees. This book attempts to acquaint the undergraduate degree holder to a variety of professional options that might be best termed working sociologist positions. Research, because of the critical nature of both the process and outcomes, is, in most cases, going to be done under the authority of someone with a master's or doctoral degree in sociology or a related field.

Supervision has marvelous advantages for the new college graduate. It allows you to learn and, therefore, to make mistakes without the full burden of responsibility. If your supervisor is a professional, it means a work situation with opportunities to learn and grow with the assurance that you are meeting generally recognized professional standards.

Because supervision involves hiring, evaluating, and training, your opportunity to observe a professional researcher/manager will provide countless examples of people management styles that you can consider in anticipation of one day being in the same situation.

The idea of a leadership role for yourself in the future is what often spurs a worker to seek the education and experience needed to take a research management or directorship role. If you work hard in your new position and learn as much as you can, you may become frustrated that you cannot make more decisions on your own. This means that it is time to move on in your career and take the necessary professional development steps to make it happen.

The Right Qualifications

A sociology degree can provide the necessary credential for you to pursue entry-level positions in research and data analysis. Still, it's one thing to have a degree, but quite another to know your research field well, especially at the entry level.

Generally, employers don't care whether you have built your skills in a classroom setting, at a part-time job, in an internship, or in a volunteer position. They just want to know that you will be able to do the work they are hiring you to do. Having had experience using necessary skills will certainly set you apart from the group of people who simply say they think they can do the work.

Research and data analysis can involve great creativity, intuition, and educated guesswork. Those are hard to determine in the interview process and even harder to pin down and evaluate. There are several attributes that go into the skill package of a research or data analysis position, and though how they are prioritized might be the subject of intense debate, most would agree on the following basic list:

- Organization
- Attention to detail
- Teaching skills
- Social skills (networking/discretion)
- Curiosity (for general information)

Organization
Check out a busy researcher's office and somewhere—on a desk, on the wall, on the computer screen—you are likely to discover a tracking chart of all

ongoing projects and their individual stages of completion. Seldom is there the luxury of having only one project; there are usually many projects. The atmosphere may not be exactly chaotic, but it won't remind you of a library, either. It's more like the newsroom of a major daily right before press time. You may well ask, "Why not just work straight through on one assignment, finish it, and move on to the next?" The reason for this should give you significant insight into the nature of research work.

Often, the researcher or data analyst cannot immediately acquire the materials or data he or she needs and must seek the help of another information specialist to provide that. This may involve letters, fax transmissions, e-mail, or telephone calls to anywhere in the world. Delays may occur, as these individuals have their own agenda, and they, in turn, may need to seek out additional information. Keeping track of these requests and the projects they relate to can be a task in itself. It even has a name—traffic management.

A library provides an excellent illustration of the need for organization. It also serves as an analogy for the work and role of the information specialist in any organization. A library, especially a large collection, is almost useless without the order imposed on it by indexing, cataloging, shelving, and retrieval systems. The newest in online catalogs provides the user with a book's location and availability. Without the system created by librarians (who can also function as researchers or data analysts), a library would be chaos and of very little use despite its potential.

But librarians do more than just order and shelve their collections. They create systems for sharing material between collections. Interlibrary loans are a good example of the librarian's ability to provide what he or she doesn't have by establishing sharing networks with those that do. Newer consortia of libraries often share databases and allow users to search the catalogs of other collections for material or references they require.

Simply put, the job of the researcher or data analyst is to connect the information seeker with the desired information. It sounds simple. But it is a complex task, one demanding all of the sociology graduate's skills to perform efficiently, quickly, and at low cost.

Every part of your job in research and data interpretation cries out for organization. Organizing your resources, time, and priorities to fulfill the information requests you receive will make constant and ever-increasing demands on your organizational ability. How frustrating and wasteful to be asked for something you've done before and yet can no longer locate, necessitating an entire repeat search. Organization is a requisite for anyone entering this field.

Attention to Detail

The researcher or data analyst wants to provide exactly the information clients request. "Almost" or "close" isn't good enough for the professional. If someone wants to know how many teenage girls pierce their ears, facts about ear piercing in women eighteen to twenty-five years old isn't going to fit the bill. You will need to dig deeper and find statistics on an age population of thirteen to nineteen years old to satisfy this request. The specialist is precise about facts for two reasons. First, clients are going to make decisions based on the information provided to them by the information resource. Second, these decisions will ultimately have an effect on the viability of the organization and its ability to stay in business and keep you, the research specialist, employed.

Social Skills

Certain social skills, such as listening, questioning, and determining others' needs, are vital. As a researcher or data analyst, you will be interacting with people constantly to best ascertain their information needs. Your possession of strong interpersonal skills will help you work more quickly and precisely. To communicate successfully with a variety of people, you will need an easy-to-understand vocabulary and, sometimes, visual aids.

Working conditions will involve lots of partnerships and cooperation with others in a variety of fields. Your networks of contacts will be vital, and your day will include much telephone and computer work and probably a fair amount of written correspondence. The importance of good written and oral communication skills cannot be emphasized enough.

Confidentiality is another important skill required in social research and data analysis. In research on topics such as the safe-sex practices of gay men, a new line of children's dolls based on a much-loved storybook character, or the indictment of a major political figure, you should easily discern the importance of confidentiality.

With top-level access to privileged information in any organization and first-look privileges at potentially sensitive or powerful findings, it is essential that you be trusted and valued for your confidentiality and discretion.

Earnings

To get a handle on the possible earnings range or spread for an entry-level information specialist, you will need to look at these positions (by whatever job title) across the full spectrum of possible employment sites (nonprofit, business/industry, education, libraries, and so forth) as well as by type of research or analysis being undertaken.

Salaries earned by analysts vary according to the type of position, along with being influenced by factors such as previous experience, type of employer, and geographical area. According to the U.S. Department of Labor, median annual earnings in 2006 were as follows for specific types of analysts:

Survey researchers: $33,360
Market research analysts: $58,820
Wage and salary management analysts: $68,050
Operations research analysts: $64,650

If you bring to your first position some specific information-management experience, better-than-average computer skills, and strong documentation of these abilities, you can expect your entry-level salary to more closely approximate the high end of a stated range. For stated entry-level salaries, you may be able to negotiate as much as 10 percent more with exceptional experience.

Career Outlook

In determining the future needs for social research and data analysis, you will immediately encounter a research challenge of your own. For example, let's look at one specific job title, that of market research analyst. These individuals—who most often work in business and industry—are charged with seeking growth opportunities for their firms by tracking new and growing markets, suggesting the discontinuing of no-longer-viable products, recommending product changes to correspond to new needs and uses, and developing initiatives to respond to competition in the marketplace.

Because the competitive marketplace is increasingly volatile and the global market a reality, information sourcing and data analysis have become crucial aspects of marketing strategy. Jobs in this business sector for researchers and data analysts will continue to be in high demand in the foreseeable future. On the other hand, these positions require that the sociology graduate arrive at business and industry's doorstep with a correspondingly complete set of skills. The very same business climate that demands researchers and data analysts stay competitive demands competitive qualifications of their applicants.

In academics, a large part of the research workload is undertaken by graduate students and faculty. In an environment that prizes the graduate degree, it is a challenge for a new job candidate with a bachelor's degree to find a spot. Nevertheless, with diligence you can find an entry-level research position that may include tuition benefits to advance your education and qualifications. Positions in academia are expected to grow at an average rate over the next ten years.

In the human services field itself, research and data analyst positions are often embedded within other job titles and, consequently, hard to identify and track. Because of the numbers of college graduates entering the helping professions at every degree level, it is expected that even with the anticipated growth in agencies and organizations dealing with social issues, supply will exceed demand and growth will be average or slightly slower than average over the next ten years.

It's not advisable to design a career strategy based on supply and demand. After all, these estimates are based on aggregate numbers, and you are looking for just one job. Nevertheless, it's a good idea to have your eyes wide open about job probabilities in whatever field you ultimately choose. But, regardless of what the experts say about your chances, if you are truly interested in a particular area and have a résumé that will get you in the door for an interview, by all means go for it.

The underlying point in any discussion of job outlook is the issues of competitiveness and the fit between your particular combination of skills and attributes and those the employer is seeking. To ensure the brightest outlook possible for your career in social research and data analysis, not just for your first job but for your continued employment in a changing market, remember one thing: use your present situation to acquire as many portable skills as possible. Portable skills go with you from job to job.

If you are still in college, tap into your college's computer services and learn as much as you can. Meet all of your sociology professors and learn about their career histories and their research interests. Get their views on the job market. Meet and talk, in person or by telephone, to as many alumni as you can who are working in sociology-related careers to hear their views on the best job preparation and hiring needs in their fields. Do an internship, if at all possible, that focuses on research or data analysis—even if the content area is outside sociology. Your experience with research methods or software systems is more portable than the topic of the research.

Once on the job, use this same advice. Meet and get to know your colleagues. Find out what their research interests may be. Take advantage of all your benefits. Attend professional development workshops, seminars, and conferences if you can. If your employer provides some sort of educational benefit, use it. Take courses that will make you a more valuable employee not only right now, but in the future, as well.

Though it may be a challenge to sum up the career outlook for all the possible research and data analyst opportunities available to you at graduation, it is no exaggeration to say that the career outlook is brightest for those who know and take full advantage of their current opportunities.

Strategy for Finding the Jobs

Perhaps the best test of your research potential would be to leave this section out of the chapter! Research positions and data analyst jobs are prevalent but widely dispersed across the employment spectrum. A good-sized organization, for example, might only have one researcher and one data analyst, or the two jobs might be combined. Locating these positions is difficult because they could be in the marketing, human resources, customer relations, or computer services department. You can enhance your job prospects by incorporating the considerations described in this section into your efforts.

Networking is essential for understanding the breadth of occupational opportunities available to you and for hearing firsthand about working conditions and hiring considerations. A college is perhaps the best place to start networking because you have an immediate network of alumni who share the common bond of your alma mater. There should be many graduates in sociology who have gone ahead of you to careers such as the one you seek. Be certain to check with your career office about connecting with these alumni.

The tremendous variety of research positions available in many different settings argues strongly for making some decisions that focus your search. It would be difficult to master the specific vocabulary, concerns, and issues of any one area if each week you were interviewing everywhere from cancer research facilities to doll manufacturers. Use your reading, networking with faculty and alumni, and information interviewing to help you sharpen your focus on one, two, or three of the job areas listed in this chapter.

One networking technique—informational interviewing—has sometimes gotten some very bad press. Too many career experts have suggested job candidates use the pretense of an informational interview to present themselves as candidates for a job. At the same time that this duplicitous strategy began to be used with increasing frequency, managers in organizations were doing more work with fewer resources. They were less inclined to offer job seekers any kind of an interview, much less an informational interview.

In some organizations, however, there is an appreciation that informational interviewing helps to raise the overall knowledge and education of the job seeker. The more aware the job seeker, the better the employment candidate.

Everyone who hires understands he or she must play a part to raise the general employability of the market.

Those seeking informational interviews have become more candid, as well. They now know to frankly express where they are in their job search and what they hope to accomplish in the informational interview. They put their cards on the table and nobody's time is wasted.

Another new twist on the informational interviewing is using your own alumni network. Most colleges maintain networks of alumni, some specifically for career information. Talk to your alumni director, explain the kinds of alumni you want to talk with and why, and see if he or she can help.

Once you have an opportunity to sit down and talk with professional researchers or data analysts, ask about how they hire for entry-level jobs. What education background and qualifications are they seeking? After you talk with these professionals, you will have a better sense of the kinds of information specialties that seem to match your interests and talents.

Informational interviewing will help you gather more information about jobs and work environments. For example, library work is often thought of as being solitary and in a very quiet setting. Talk with a professional to uncover the realities. Library staff members do have fun, and teamwork is critical to their success. Advertising is often thought of as a busy, hectic, and unconventional industry. Information specialists working in this industry may find themselves very busy indeed, but the work is often not as glamorous as some believe it is. No matter what type of work or work setting you are considering, find out what it is really like. Talk with other entry-level employees as well as seasoned veterans to get the complete picture, so you can better judge for yourself whether that setting would be a good place to work.

Finding a Focus

To build a career as an information specialist, you will have to—at a fairly early stage in your career—make a decision about how you want to specialize. You will certainly be able to gain an entry-level position with a bachelor's degree, but to see career growth in an information specialty you will probably need an advanced degree. If library work interests you, for example, you would be able to obtain several types of library jobs with a bachelor's degree in sociology, but if you hope to work as a librarian, a master's degree in library science would be required. If you are interested in organizing the information gathered by a large corporation, an advanced degree in information systems management or a more general master's in business administration would be needed to move into upper levels of management.

So how do you begin to decide what to specialize in? Part-time work, summer jobs, and internships are all employment opportunities you can use while you are in school. They can help you see what various environments are like and what type of people work in each setting, as well as to gain a deeper understanding of the nature of the work.

Internet sites such as Internships.com, Internweb.com, and Student jobs.gov are great places to locate internships. Other, more general career and job sites such as Job.com, HotJobs.com, Job-Hunt.com, Career Builder Canada, and Canadajobs.com also include internships in their job listings.

While most internships are unpaid, if you can afford to take an internship, it often breaks the cycle of "no experience, no job." You will come away from the internship with solid research experience, references from professional researchers, and a network of new acquaintances to support you in your job search upon graduation.

If you have already graduated, you may want to consider temporary or term employment opportunities. This kind of employment can be useful if you want to experience several types of jobs before you make a commitment to specialize in one area or field. Temp agencies operate in nearly every geographic location, and some of them specialize in the type of placement they make (paralegal, systems management, and so forth).

Possible Job Titles

As you search for an information specialist position, the following are some of the job titles you may encounter:

- Data analyst
- Labor force and manpower analyst
- Policy analyst
- Population analyst
- Principal investigator
- Research director
- Social science analyst
- Social survey director
- Statistical analyst
- Survey research technician

The variety and confusion of job titles should indicate several important things to the job searcher:

• The field of information specialization remains largely undefined, at least in job titles. Certainly, those who employ people to act as information specialists have not yet agreed on a common terminology. The lack of a definitive job title may also indicate individual job roles vary equally as much. People working in informational services still organize themselves by content area and not by their more general role as information networkers.

• The lack of a common job title requires you to read and carefully understand the job description for which you are applying. It is in these job duties and responsibility delineations that you will come to appreciate the focus and emphasis of that particular position and not only whether it meets your expectations of the job of an information specialist, but also whether you have the particular skill package the employer is seeking.

Professional Associations

In the following list of associations, you will find a wide range of organizations that will be able to provide additional data about particular information specialties. Review the "Members/Purpose" section for each organization and decide whether the organization pertains to your interests. Membership in one organization may well be worth the investment in terms of networking opportunities, job listings, or placement services. Remember, some organizations will provide limited career information at no charge, but if you want to receive publications that often include job listings, you must actually join the organization. Many, however, have greatly reduced membership dues for full-time students.

American Consultants League
c/o ETR
245 Northeast Fourth Avenue
Delray Beach, FL 22483
Members/Purpose: Full- and part-time consultants in varied fields of expertise.
Publications: *Consulting Intelligence*, newsletters, directory
Training: Offers a certification program
Job Listings: None

American Library Association (ALA)
50 East Huron Street
Chicago, IL 60611
ala.org

Members/Purpose: Librarians, libraries, trustees, friends of libraries, and others interested in the responsibilities of libraries in the educational and cultural needs of society.

Publications: ALA handbook of organization, membership directory, *American Libraries, Booklist, ALA TechSource, Book Links, Choice*

Job Listings: Offers placement services; see American Libraries for listings

American Society for Information Science and Technology (ASIS&T)
1320 Fenwick Lane, Suite 510
Silver Spring, MD 20910
asis.org

Members/Purpose: Information specialists, scientists, librarians, administrators, social scientists, and others interested in the use, organization, storage, retrieval, evaluation, and dissemination of recorded specialized information.

Publications: *Annual Review of Information Science and Technology, Bulletin,* handbook and directory, *Jobline, Journal of the American Society for Information Science and Technology,* conference proceedings

Training: Conducts continuing education programs and professional development workshops

Job Listings: Maintains placement service; see online Jobline

Association for Operations Management
5301 Shawnee Road
Alexandria, VA 23212
apics.org

Members/Purpose: Organization of professionals in various areas of systems and operations management.

Publication: *APICS Magazine*

Training: Offers professional development opportunities in operations management

Job Listings: Offers online career center

Association for Research on Nonprofit Organizations and Voluntary Actions (ARNOVA)
340 West Michigan Street
Indianapolis, IN 46202
arnova.org

Members/Purpose: Stimulates, coordinates, and aids the efforts of those engaged in voluntary action research, scholarship, and professional activity.

Publications: *Nonprofit and Voluntary Sector Quarterly, ARNOVA News,*
occasional papers
Training: Sponsors collaborative research proposals and projects on
voluntary action topics
Job Listings: None

Association of American Publishers (AAP)
71 Fifth Avenue
New York, NY 10003
publishers.org
Members/Purpose: Trade association representing producers of hardbound
and softbound general, educational, trade, reference, religious, scientific,
technical, and medical books; instructional materials; classroom
periodicals; maps, globes, tests, and software.
Publications: Offers a wide range of publications including annual report,
The Copyright Primer, and marketing reports on the publishing industry
Training: Conducts seminars and workshops on various publishing topics,
including rights and permissions sales, and educational publishing
Job Listings: Lists job openings online under Bookjobs.com; also lists
internships

Canadian Marketing Association (CMA)
1 Concorde Gate, Suite 607
Don Mills, ON M3C 3N6
the-cma.org
Members/Purpose: Operates as the largest marketing association in
Canada, serving approximately eight hundred corporate members,
including major financial institutions, insurance companies, publishers,
retailers, charitable organizations, and others with an interest in
marketing.
Publications: *Activities & Accomplishments, E-Communicator Newsletter,
Weekly Watching Brief,* member bulletins and briefings, *Marketing Fact Book*
Training: Offers Professional Marketing certificates, courses in areas such as
direct marketing and relationship marketing, national conventions, one-
day conferences
Job Listings: None

National Science Foundation (NSF)
4201 Wilson Boulevard
Arlington, VA 22230
nsf.gov

Members/Purpose: Independent agency in the executive branch concerned primarily with the support of basic and applied research and education in the sciences and engineering. Funds scientific research in many areas, including social science research.

Publications: Annual report, *NSF Current* newsletter, policy newsletter, many others in fields such as biology, engineering, geosciences, and other fields

Training: Supports various education and training efforts through federal funding

Job Listings: Lists openings within the agency online; also provides link to USAJOBS

Society for Nonprofit Organizations (SNPO)

5820 Canton Center Road, Suite 165
Canton, MI 48187
snpo.org

Members/Purpose: Executive directors, staff, board members, volunteers, and other professionals who serve nonprofit organizations.

Publications: *Nonprofit World, National Directory of Service/Product Providers, Funding Alert*

Training: Sponsors seminars and workshops on nonprofit management and leadership

Job Listings: Offers online job information

Special Libraries Association (SLA)

331 South Patrick Street
Alexandria, VA 22314
sla.org

Members/Purpose: International association of information professionals who work in special libraries serving business, research, government, universities, newspapers, museums, and institutions that use or produce specialized information.

Publications: *Information Outlook Online*, e-newsletters, chapter and division publications

Training: Conducts continuing education courses

Job Listings: Offers online career center

Further Reading

AHA Guide to U.S. Hospitals, Health Care Systems, Networks, Alliances, Health Organizations, Agencies, & Providers. Chicago: American Hospital Association, 2008.

The Book of U.S. Government Jobs: Where They Are, What's Available & How to Get One. McKees Rocks, PA: Bookhaven Press, 2008.

Biech, Elaine. *The Business of Consulting: The Basics and Beyond.* San Francisco: Pfeiffer, 2007.

Bobrow Burns, Jennifer. *Career Opportunities in the Nonprofit Sector.* New York: Checkmark Books, 2006.

Campbell, David. *If You Don't Know Where You're Going, You'll Probably End Up Somewhere Else: Finding a Career and Getting a Life.* Notre Dame, IN: Sorin Books, 2007.

Canter, Rachelle J. *Make the Right Career Move: 28 Critical Insights and Strategies to Land Your Dream Job.* Hoboken, NJ: Wiley, 2006.

Careers in Nonprofits and Government Agencies. Philadelphia: WetFeet, Inc., 2006.

Eikleberry, Carol. *Career Guide for Creative and Unconventional People.* Berkeley, CA: Ten Speed Press, 2007.

Encyclopedia of Associations. Detroit: Gale Cenage, 2007.

Fredericks, Anthony. *The Complete Idiot's Guide to Teaching College.* Royersfield, PA: Alpha, 2007.

Gassner, Laura. *Change Your Career: Transitioning to the Nonprofit Sector.* New York: Kaplan Publishing, 2007.

Harrington, Brad, and Douglas T. Hall. *Career Management & Work-Life Integration: Using Self-Assessment to Navigate Contemporary Careers.* Los Angeles: Sage Publications, 2007.

Lauber, Daniel. *Government Job Finder: Where the Jobs Are in Local, State, and Federal Government.* River Forest, IL: Planning Communications, 2008.

Lerner, Marcy. *Vault Guide to the Top Government and Non-Profit Legal Employers.* New York: Vault, Inc., 2003.

Marke, Rosanne J. *Opportunities in Social Science Careers.* Chicago: McGraw-Hill, 2004.

McKinney, Anne. *Real Resumes for Jobs in Nonprofit Organizations.* Fayetteville, NC: Prep Publishing, 2004.

Stephens, Richard. *Careers in Sociology.* Cranbury, NJ: Allyn & Bacon, 2003.

Strayer, Susan. *The Right Job, Right Now: The Complete Toolkit for Finding Your Perfect Career.* New York: St. Martin's Griffin, 2006.

Sweet, Stephen. *Changing Contours of Work: Jobs and Opportunities in the New Economy.* Los Angeles: Pine Forge Press, 2007.

Walsh, Richard. *The Complete Job Search Book for College Students: A Step-by-Step Guide to Finding the Right Job.* Cincinnati: Adams Media Corporation, 2007.

What to Do with Your Psychology or Sociology Degree. New York: Princeton Review, 2007.

Index

www.ingramcontent.com/pod-product-compliance
Lightning Source LLC
Chambersburg PA
CBHW060334100426
42812CB00003B/992